Editor
Kathy Humrichouse

Editorial Project Manager
Paul Gardner

Editor in Chief
Sharon Coan, M.S. Ed.

Creative Director
Elayne Roberts

Product Manager
Phil Garcia

Imaging
Alfred Lau

Acknowledgements:
Netscape logos and trademarks are
reproduced with the expressed written
consent of Netscape Communications
Corporation. Netscape, Netscape
Certificater Server, Netscape FastTrack
Server, Netscape Navigator, Netscape
ONE, SuiteSpot, and the Netscape N and
Ship's Wheel logos are registered
trademarks of Netscape Communications
Corporation in the United States and other
countries. Netscape® Composer,
Netscape® Collabra®, Netscape®
Communicator, Netscape® Messenger,
and Netscape Navigator® are also
trademarks of Netscape Communications
Corporation, which may be registered in
other countries.

Publishers:
Rachelle Cracchiolo, M.S. Ed.
Mary Dupuy Smith, M.S. Ed.

Netscape
for
Terrified Teachers

Author

Debi Hooper

Teacher Created Materials, Inc.
6421 Industry Way
Westminster, CA 92683
www.teachercreated.com
ISBN-1-57690-445-8
©2000 Teacher Created Materials, Inc.
Made in U.S.A.

Table of Contents

Table of Contents *(cont.)*

Introduction

You have been hearing about the Net, e-mail, newsgroups, graphics, multimedia, and teleconferencing. Now that you have access to the Internet and this software package, where do you start? Welcome to *Netscape Communicator,* one of the leading access suites for the Internet. With this software package, you will be able to do all of those things and more.

This book will lead you through all of the components of the *Netscape* software suite and explain how you can use the components within your classroom. There will be step-by-step instructions for setting up your *Netscape* utilities and for accessing resources on the Internet to use with your curriculum.

The *Netscape Communicator* suite has four components that are integrated, or work together, to provide you with access to the Internet's resources.

Navigator—This component is one you will probably use most often. It is your Web browser or the software you will use to access Web pages on the World Wide Web.

Messenger—This is your e-mail (or electronic mail) and newsgroup software component. You will use it to exchange messages with other Internet users. By setting up newsgroups, you will be able to access messages from groups of other Internet users about a variety of subjects. There are hundreds of newsgroups about special topics and software packages.

Conference—With this utility, you can conference with other teachers and classes around the world. If you have a camera and microphone attached to your computer, you can see and talk with them as well.

Composer—You can use this component to help you design and publish your own Web pages. It is a HyperText Markup Language, or HTML, editor. You can create your pages "from scratch" or use the Wizards.

Using This Book

This book will be divided according to *Netscape Communicator's* components. Within each section, you will read directions for setting up and using the component, and there will be suggestions for integrating its use into your curriculum.

To help you or provide you with reminders as you work through this book, these graphics will mark items of interest.

 Note:—There will be notes throughout the book which will be reminders or will direct you to instructions in other parts of the book.

 Web page—You will be advised to key in different URLs or Uniform Resource Locators (Web page addresses).

 Help—This icon will direct you to more information about a topic or help with instructions all through the book.

The following font styles will be used as guides throughout the book.

Bold Italic Words in bold italic will show you which menu items you should click as you follow directions.

Italic Items in italic are words you will be asked to key in.

 Note: The instructions and graphics in this book will apply to *Netscape Communicator* for *Windows '95*. The instructions should be the same or similar for Macintosh users.

Using the Internet

What is the Internet? If your school has a network, then you have already experienced something similar to the Internet. A network is simply a group of computers connected to each other by cables. This is done so that they can all access one main computer (called a file server) and share files. This type of network is called a LAN or local area network.

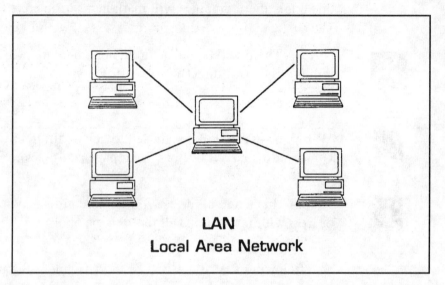

LAN
Local Area Network

If your building's network is also connected to other buildings in your school district, then you have a WAN or wide area network.

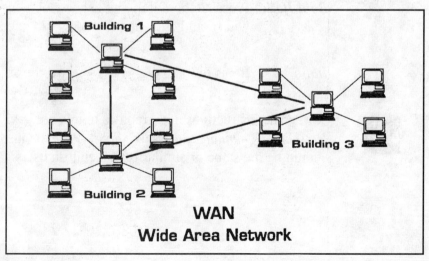

WAN
Wide Area Network

Using the Internet *(cont.)*

This is exactly what the Internet is. It is a large network of computers and file servers in different buildings, cities, states, and countries. The cables that connect these computers range from fiber optic cables to twisted copper cables to telephone lines.

There are two basic ways for you to be connected to the Internet. The first way is by dialing an Internet service provider or ISP. To do this, you must have a modem in your computer and an account with a provider. The second way is to be wired to the Internet through your school's network. In either instance, your access to the Internet through *Netscape*'s software will be the same.

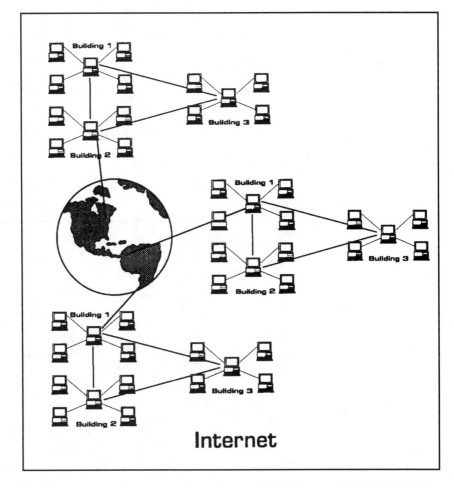

About Netscape

Netscape was founded in April, 1994 by Dr. James H. Clark, founder of Silicon Graphics, and Marc Andreessen, creator of NCSA *Mosaic* software that was the first graphical Internet browser.

In October of that year, *Netscape* developed an innovative way of distributing their software. They made the first copies of *Netscape Navigator* client software available for downloading from their Web site on the Internet.

The *Netscape* software continues to be free in beta version to the general public and free to anyone working in the education field. The following Web site is for downloading and upgrades.

http://home.netscape.com/computing/download/index.html

The *Netscape* Web site is now the busiest site in the world with close to five million users. It receives more than 120 million visits (or hits) each day. You can visit the *Netscape* Web site at this address to find information, logo products, and additional software.

http://home.netscape.com

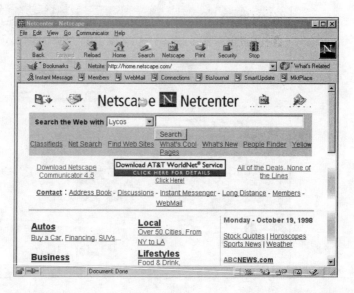

Starting Out

The component of this software that you will use most often is *Netscape's Navigator*. *Navigator* is your World Wide Web browser. This is the software that will connect you to Web pages around the world. You will be able to keep bookmarks of your favorite Web sites, download files, and view graphics and multimedia.

 To start *Navigator*, double-click the **Navigator** icon on your desktop or in the *Netscape* folder.

As the program starts, you will see this splash screen showing the status of *Navigator* as it is loading your bookmarks and plug-ins.

Navigator will open to *Netscape*'s home page where you will be able to search for information, download upgrades, check your Web mail, and locate information from several basic groupings of topics.

Navigator Window

The following elements are contained in the *Netscape* window.

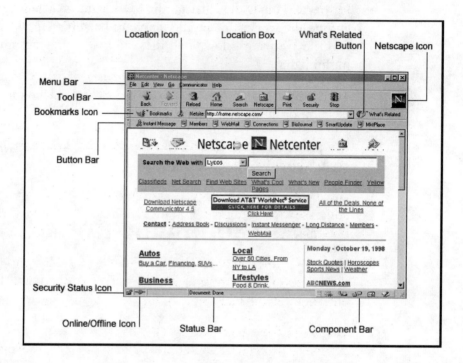

Menu Bar—Like other programs, this bar appears at the top of the window and contains menus from which you can choose instructions for the program.

Tool Bar—This tool bar provides you with buttons to make your browsing easier. You will be able to click to go back to a previous page, go to the next page, reload pages, stop loading pages, etc.

Bookmarks Icon—This icon, or button, opens your list of bookmarks or favorite Web pages.

Location Icon—This icon can be used to create a new bookmark or button from a current Web page location.

Navigator Window *(cont.)*

Location Box—This text box shows the address (URL—Uniform Resource Locator) of the current Web page. You can key a Web page address into this box to go to that specific page.

What's Related Button—This button will search through *Netscape's* database of related sites and provide you with a short list of sites similar to the one you are currently viewing.

Netscape Icon—This icon shows shooting stars as *Navigator* is loading a Web page. You can also click this button to immediately go to *Netscape's* home page.

Button Bar—This bar displays buttons for the Web page addresses that are located in the Personal Toolbar Folder of your bookmarks.

Security Status Icon—This icon shows you the security level of the page you are currently viewing. This is important if you are entering personal data at a Web site.

Online/Offline Icon—You can click this icon or button to go offline to use your browser or other components of Netscape.

Status Bar—This bar shows the current loading status of a Web page. It will display the percentage of the page that is finished downloading and any attached graphics, sound, or multimedia files that are loading. It will also display the address, or URL, of any hyperlink you move your mouse across while viewing a Web page.

Component Bar—This bar contains buttons for quickly changing to other components of *Communicator*. It will appear in the lower right-hand corner of each component so you can easily switch back and forth.

Tool Bar

Take a closer look at the button options on *Navigator*'s tool bar.

As you are browsing through Web pages, you will be able to click the ***Back*** button to return to previously viewed pages.

After viewing previous pages, you can click the ***Forward*** button to move forward in the series of viewed pages.

You can click the ***Reload*** button to refresh the current Web page if your transfer was interrupted for some reason.

You can click the ***Home*** button to return to whichever Web page you have designated as your home page. The default setting that was installed with the software returns you to *Netscape*'s home page.

Tool Bar *(cont.)*

When you click the *Search* button, you will see the **Netscape Netcenter** search engine Web page.

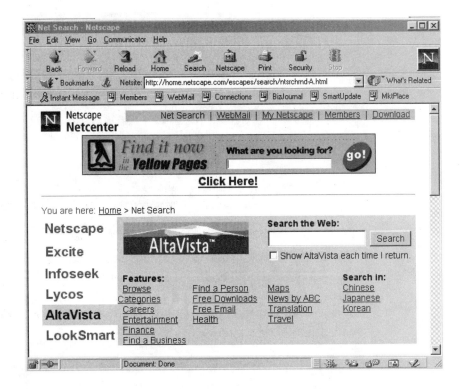

This will allow you to choose from several search sites to assist you in finding other Web pages. The **Net Search** Web page is a central location for many of the major search engine sites.

© *Teacher Created Materials, Inc.*   13   *#2445 Netscape for Terrified Teachers*

Tool Bar *(cont.)*

The *My Netscape* button takes you to **Netscape Netcenter's My Netscape** Web page.

Once you have registered with **Netscape's Netcenter**, you can log on to **My Netscape** and set up your own page design. You can also designate this Web page to be the home page that appears when you click the *Home* button.

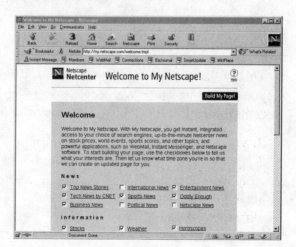

Tool Bar *(cont.)*

By clicking the *Print* button, you can easily print the Web page you are currently viewing.

When you click the *Security* button, you can view detailed information about the Web page that you are viewing.

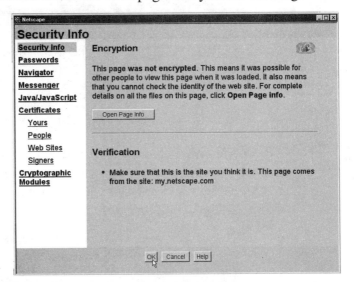

If you need to stop a Web page from loading, you can click the *Stop* button. There will be times when the connection between you and a Web page may be slow. Instead of waiting for a Web page to load, you can simply click this button and then go to a different Web page.

Menu Bar

The menu bar on the *Netscape* components gives you options for printing and viewing Web pages. You will use menu selections to insert your e-mail and newsgroup settings and to set other preferences. This will be an overview of the menu bar selections. Many of the menu selections will be the same in each of the *Netscape* components.

By clicking each of the words on the menu bar, you will see a menu of additional choices drop down.

File Menu

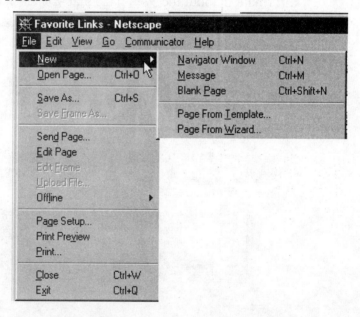

If you click *File* and *New*, you will see a menu of new items you can open on your screen. The first item is another *Navigator* window. If you are viewing a Web page and want to go to another Web page without losing your place on the first page, you can choose to open another *Navigator* window. You can also choose to open a new *Navigator* window if you are working with another *Netscape* component.

Menu Bar *(cont.)*

If you click *File*, then *New*, then *Message*, you will open the mail *Messenger* window with a blank message screen available for you to write an e-mail.

Choosing *File*, then *New*, then *Blank Page* will open a blank document in the *Composer* component. You can use *Composer* to create a Web page.

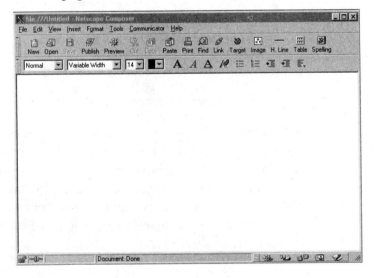

Menu Bar *(cont.)*

The *File*, then *New*, then *Page From Template* choice will allow you to use template (or pre-made) files from the *Netscape* Web site.

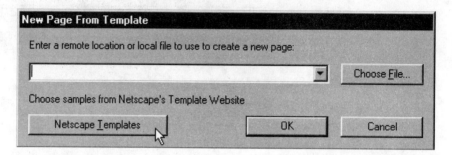

When you click the *Netscape Templates* button, your browser will travel to the *Netscape* Web site, and you will see a list of possible files.

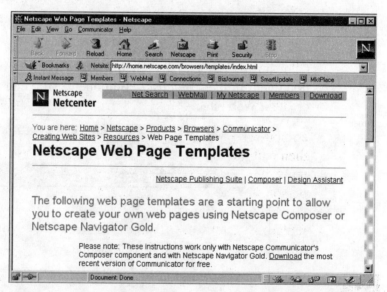

There are many template choices created by professionals at *Netscape*, and you can edit them within your *Composer* window. You can then upload them to your choice of Web sites, or you can publish them on your school's network.

Menu Bar *(cont.)*

Browse through the list of choices and click the link to a page you would like to view.

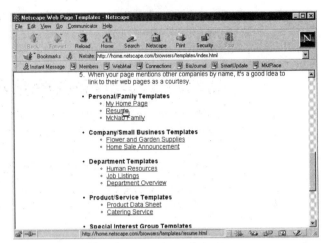

If you select the ***Résumé*** choice, you will see a sample Web page résumé. There are instructions for saving this page to your computer and then editing it to make it personal. Once you have

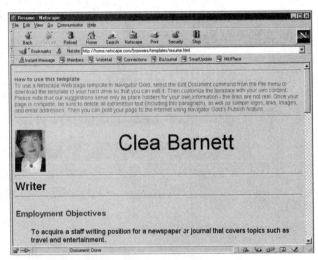

replaced the text and graphics with your own, you can download the Web page or e-mail it to someone.

Note: The template files would be a good place for you and your students to start when you begin to create a Web page project. You can also use the résumé Web page to document the workshops and training you are completing as a teacher.

Menu Bar *(cont.)*

If you have Web pages saved on your computer, you can use the *File*, *Open Page* selection to open and view those Web pages in your *Navigator* window.

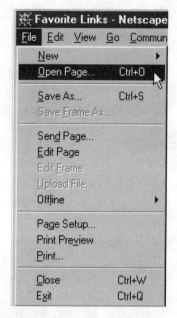

You will see this dialog box. You can either key in the filename of the Web page or click the *Choose File* button to browse through the folders and files on your computer.

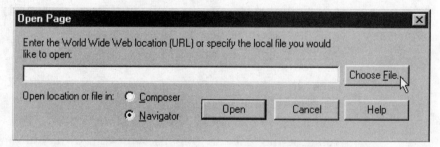

You can select whether you want to open a file in the *Navigator* window to view it or the *Composer* window to edit it.

Menu Bar *(cont.)*

If you click the ***Choose File*** button, you will get a dialog box in which you can browse through the files on your computer and select the file you want to open.

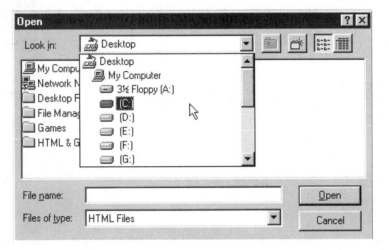

You can click the ***Open*** button on this dialog box and then click the ***Open*** button on the previous dialog box.

If you find a Web page online that you want to keep on your computer for reference, you can use the ***Save As*** command.

This will save the HTML file. It will not save graphics or other multimedia files that are included with the Web page.

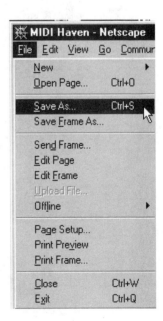

You can use this option to save one of the *Netscape* template Web pages. You can then open the saved file and edit it. You can also use this option to rename the template file as you save it.

Menu Bar *(cont.)*

If the Web page is divided into sections called frames, you can use the ***Save Frame As*** command to save the frame document as an HTML file.

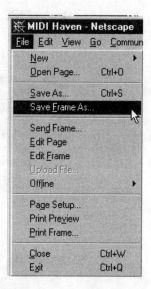

By selecting ***Save As*** or ***Save Frame As***, you will see a dialog box which allows you to save the file in the folder of your choice.

Note: It is a good idea to create a separate folder in which you will save your Web pages. It will make it much easier to find them later.

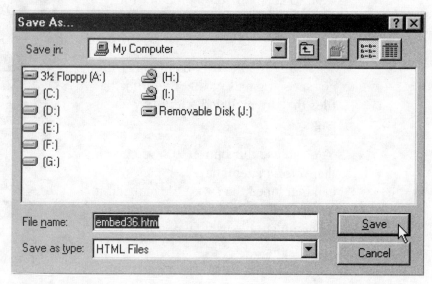

Menu Bar *(cont.)*

If you are viewing a Web page and would like to quickly send the address to someone else, you can click *File*, *Send Page*. If you are viewing a Web page with frames, you will be given the choice to *Send Frame*.

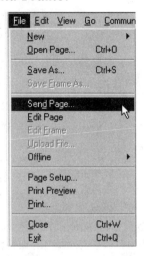 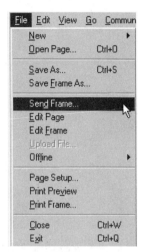

When you select one of these commands, your messenger window will appear with the Web page address, or URL (Uniform Resource Locator), already entered in a new e-mail message.

Menu Bar *(cont.)*

If you are viewing a Web page in your *Navigator* window and want to edit it, you can select *File*, *Edit Page*.

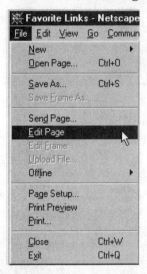

This will open the Web page in your *Composer* window. You will then be able to edit it and re-save it.

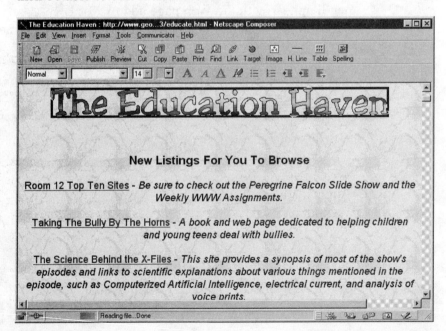

Menu Bar *(cont.)*

If you want to work on Web pages while you are offline, you can click *File*, *Offline*, *Work Offline*. This will allow you to keep your browser window open while you are offline.

Note: If you are working with an offline browser program, such as *Web Buddy*, you can read the downloaded Web pages in your *Navigator* window while offline. You can also use this option at school if you do not have online access from your classroom computer.

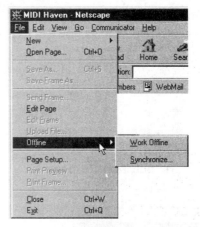

The *Synchronize* command can be used to reorganize all of your work once you get back online. E-mail will be sent and Web pages can be uploaded. This saves you actual online time.

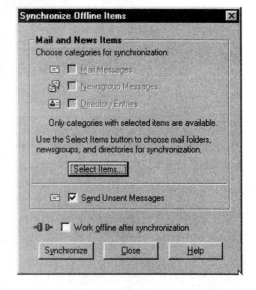

Menu Bar *(cont.)*

Quite often, you will want to print a hard copy of a Web page so you can read it later or use it in your classroom. By clicking *File*, *Page Setup*, you can select several printing options. The *Page Setup* dialog box will be different for each printer, but the options will be similar.

Select black text when printing Web pages with light or white colored text on a dark background. If you try to print light-colored text, you may not be able to read the text.

This also applies to hypertext link colors. Look at them carefully before printing so you can choose black text on the hard copy if they are light in color on the Web page.

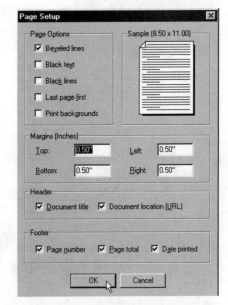

You can also select different page margins and add or delete Header and Footer information.

The default, or normal print setup, includes the document title and URL as well as page numbers and date printed.

This is important information to have if you need to remember where and when you found the information. The document title and URL are also important when citing these pages as references.

Menu Bar *(cont.)*

Before printing, it is best to view how your hard copy will look. Click *File*, *Print Preview* to see how the Web page will look when you print it.

The sample page below shows the document title and location (URL). It will also show page numbers and the date the page is printed. It will not print any background graphic.

To close the preview window and return to the browser window, click the *Close* button.

To print the page from this window, just click the *Print* button.

Menu Bar *(cont.)*

In order to print a Web page without previewing it first, simply click *File*, then *Print*.

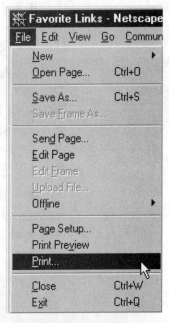

The *Print* dialog box will appear, and you will be able to select the printing options you want, such as which pages to print and how many copies you want of each page.

Note: Be sure the proper printer is selected before printing. If you will be using the Web page in the classroom, you may want to print it on transparency film. Be sure to select the *Properties* options button and then choose *Best quality* for the printing option and *Transparency Film* as the paper option.

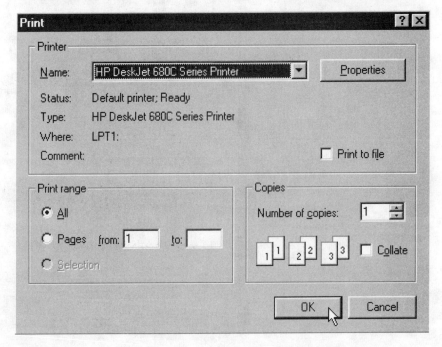

Menu Bar *(cont.)*

To close a window without exiting the program, click *File*, *Close*. This will close the selected window while leaving other *Netscape* windows open.

To exit all *Netscape* windows, click *File*, *Exit*.

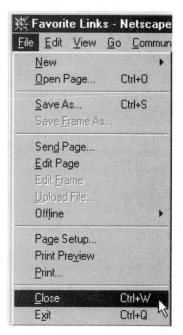 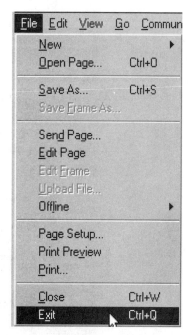

The Exit Confirmation dialog box will appear, and you will be able to click *Yes* or *No* when asked if you want to close all of the *Netscape* windows and exit *Netscape*.

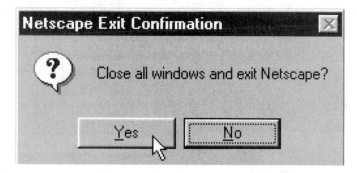

Menu Bar *(cont.)*

Edit Menu

The *Edit* menu has many options for you to utilize. Cutting, copying, and pasting work in the same way as those features in a word processing program. You can copy sections of text and paste them into documents.

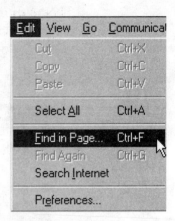

The items for you to look at now are *Find in Page*, *Search Internet*, and *Preferences*.

The *Find in Page* option allows you to search a Web page for specific text. Click *Edit* and *Find in Page*.

The *Find* dialog box will appear. Key in the text you wish to find in the document. Once you have keyed text into the blank, the *Find Next* button will become active.

Click the Find Next button to perform the search.

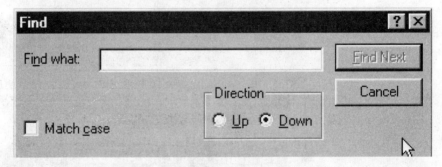

If the text appears on the Web page, *Navigator* will scroll down to that line, and the text will be highlighted.

Menu Bar *(cont.)*

The ***Search Internet*** option is the same as the ***Search*** button on the *Navigator* tool bar.

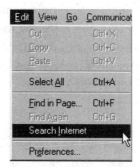

Click ***Edit***, ***Search Internet*** to go to the online search engine Web site.

Navigator will travel to the *Netscape* Netcenter where you can easily use one of several common search engines such as Excite, Infoseek, Lycos, AltaVista, or LookSmart.

Key the keywords for your search into the blank and then click the ***Search*** button.

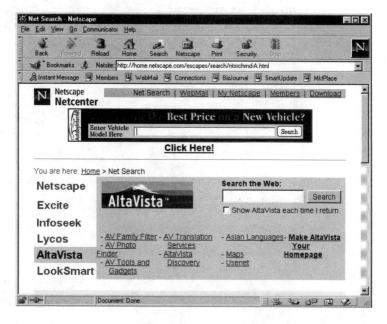

Menu Bar *(cont.)*

The *Preferences* option is what you will use to set up your *Netscape* components. From the appearance of your *Navigator* window to Mail and Newsgroup memberships, each component of *Netscape* has options you can set to personalize your *Netscape* use.

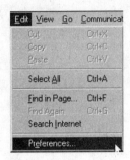

Click *Edit*, *Preferences* to set these options.

Click the *Appearance* category to make those selections. Check the boxes for the components you want to appear when you launch or start up *Netscape*. For example, choose *Navigator* if you use the World Wide Web each time you launch *Netscape*, or select *Messenger* if you check your e-mail each time you launch it.

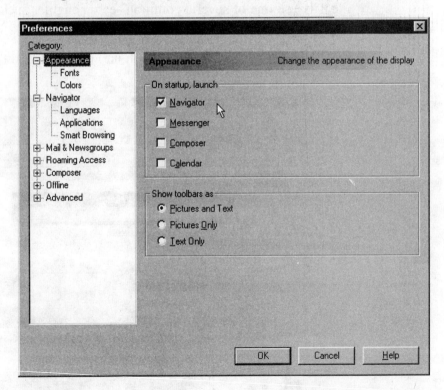

Menu Bar *(cont.)*

Click the **Fonts** category to change the appearance of your *Navigator* fonts.

If you have trouble reading the text on Web pages or have younger students who need larger type, select a larger size of type to appear on your screen.

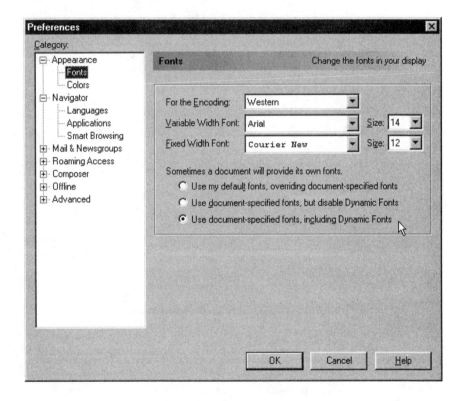

In order to make your choices always appear, click the option **Use my default fonts, overriding document-specified fonts.** This tells *Netscape* to use your choices rather than the choices specified in a Web page.

Menu Bar *(cont.)*

Click the *Colors* category to set the color preferences for viewing
Web pages.

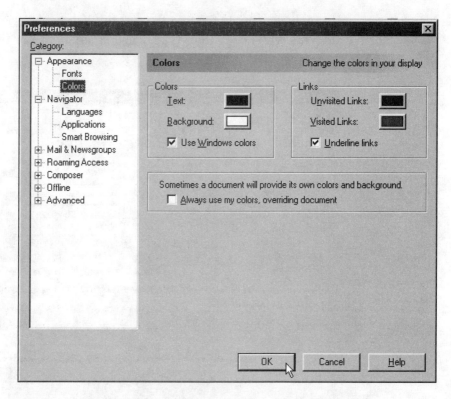

Click each color button to choose your preferences for *Text*,
Background, *Unvisited Links*, and *Visited Links*. If you want to
only view Web pages with these colors, click in the box to choose
Always use my colors, overriding document.

This is useful if you have a slow Internet connection and want to
save time while loading Web pages. The pages will use your
choices of colors rather than reading and interpreting the colors
designated by the individual Web pages. This will also save time
loading and displaying a background graphic.

Menu Bar *(cont.)*

For example, go to the Web site, **The Education Haven**, at this URL:

http://www.geocities.com/Athens/1573/educate.html

This site has a background graphic like this:

If you prefer not to view the background, you can change your color preference choice to ***Always use my colors***, ***overriding document***, and the Web page will load more quickly and look like this:

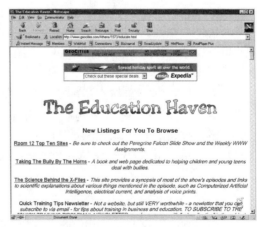

Access speed and content may be more important to you and your students than colorful background images.

Menu Bar *(cont.)*

Click *Navigator* in the preference categories.

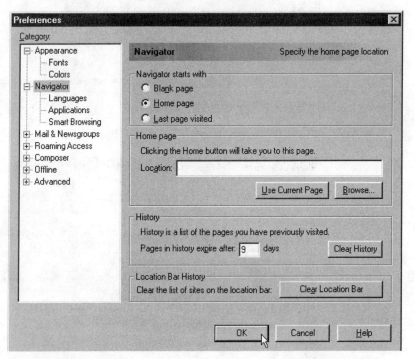

At this dialog box, you can set the page you will view when *Navigator* opens. If you are able to write your own Web page, you may want to designate that page on your computer as the opening page. It is much faster for *Navigator* to open with a page on the local computer instead of looking online for a Web page.

You can also choose to have it open with a blank page if your Internet connection is slow. This would allow you to use *Navigator* easily, even when you are not online.

History will show which Web sites you and your students have recently visited. Here you can set a specific number of days after which those history locations will be deleted from the file. You can also click the ***Clear History*** button to delete those URLs from the list.

Menu Bar *(cont.)*

The Location Bar shows the last 15 Web sites which were keyed in to *Navigator.* You can also clear those sites from your *Navigator* window by clicking the **Clear Location Bar** button. Once you have done that, key in a URL into the location bar in your *Navigator* window. This ensures that only that URL will be in the location listing. This is important to know if you are trying to clear some inappropriate URLs from the location list.

Click the **Languages** category.

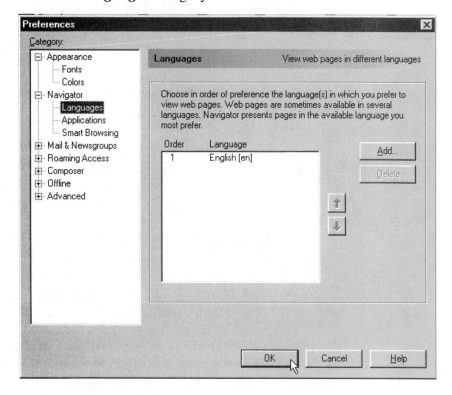

You most likely have only one language loaded into your *Netscape* folder. If, however, you have more than one, and you find that your *Netscape* components are now speaking a different language or gibberish to you, you can come here to reset the language preference.

Menu Bar *(cont.)*

Click the *Applications* category.

This is where you can manually set a program to open various files. It is usually set automatically when you install a new program or *Netscape* plug-in.

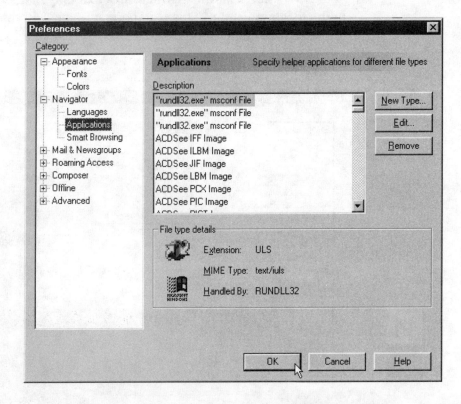

Attempting to view some files may result in a dialog box requesting that you set an associated application for viewing. You will need to be aware of which programs you have on your computer for viewing or running such files.

Note: You may have to ask your school or district technician to set additional applications for new file types.

Menu Bar *(cont.)*

Click the *Smart Browsing* category.

This is the option that uses the *What's Related* button on your *Navigator* window.

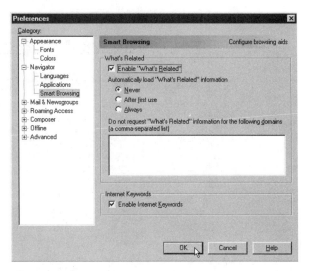

When it is enabled, you will see a button to the right of the Location Bar window.

When viewing a Web page, you can click the *What's Related* button, and *Netscape* will show you a list of other Web pages related to the topic you are viewing.

To disable the *What's Related* button, click to remove the check mark in this preference dialog box, and it will not appear when you use *Navigator*.

Menu Bar *(cont.)*

Click the **Mail & Newsgroups** category to see the preference options for *Netscape Messenger*.

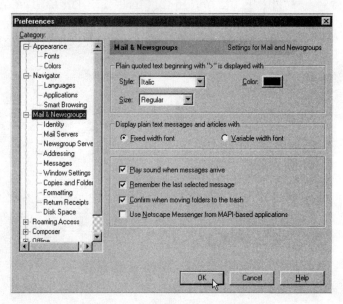

This dialog box allows you to set some simple options. First, you can choose whether you want to hear a sound file played when you receive mail. If your computer is always "up and running" when you are in the classroom, you may not want to hear an audio signal each time you receive e-mail.

Next, you can decide whether you want to have *Messenger* ask you to confirm moving mail folders to the trash. Until you get used to using *Messenger* or any e-mail program, it is best to leave that option available in case you accidentally start to delete an e-mail message.

If you have other programs that allow you to send files via e-mail, you should check the box next to **Use Netscape Messenger from MAPI-based applications**. If you are not aware of any other programs which allow you to e-mail files, just leave this box blank.

Menu Bar *(cont.)*

The *Identity* preference dialog box is the location where you set up what information will be sent to others with each of your e-mail messages.

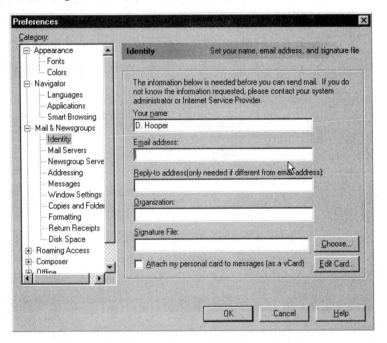

Enter your name or perhaps your classroom name into the *Your name:* box.

Key in your e-mail address so it will appear when recipients read your e-mail.

If you want recipients to reply to an e-mail address different from the one from which you are sending mail, enter the other e-mail address in the *Reply-to:* space.

If you want to specify an organization or school name, enter it in the *Organization:* space.

If you want to include general information at the bottom of all e-mail that you send, you can put it into the *Signature File:*.

Menu Bar *(cont.)*

To produce a signature file, create a document file with the information you want to include in your signature. You can use a simple editing program such as *WordPad*.

Save it to a folder that will be easy to remember. You may want to save it to the folder where your *Netscape* program is located.

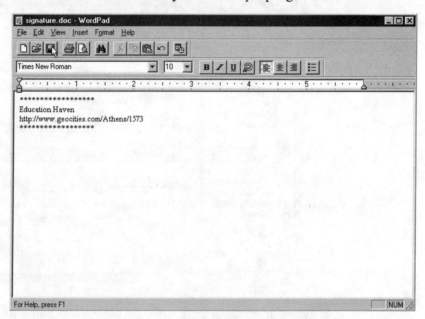

Once you have saved the signature file, you can choose it in your *Messenger* preferences. Click the **Choose** button on the **Identity** dialog box and search for the file in the file dialog box.

Once you have located your saved file, click the **Open** button to use it as your *Messenger* signature.

Menu Bar *(cont.)*

The location of the saved signature file will now appear in the Signature File space in the *Identity* dialog box.

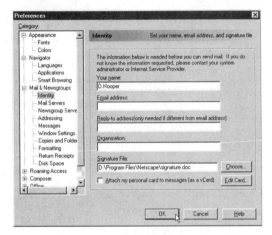

Another option in the *Identity Preferences* dialog box is the *Attach my personal card to messages* or vCard option. This will attach a virtual address/business card to an e-mail message.

Click the *Edit Card* button and fill in all appropriate blanks for the vCard. This will then be sent as an attachment to your e-mail messages.

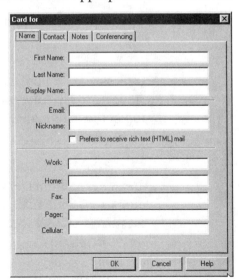

Note: Be aware that not everyone enjoys receiving attachments to e-mail messages. Newsgroups and list servers particularly do not like e-mail messages with attachments since the server then resends that message to hundreds of members.

Menu Bar *(cont.)*

Click the *Mail Servers* category.

If this has not already been set up for you by your technical support person, you will have to set up your e-mail server information.

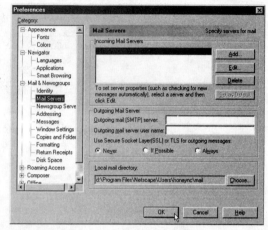

Click the *Add* button to add the information for your e-mail account.

You should also make sure a folder (directory) has been designated for storing e-mail. You can choose a different one by clicking the *Choose* button under "Local mail directory."

To set up properties such as checking automatically for e-mail, select the server and click the *Edit* button.

Fill in the Server and User names. Check the box to have *Messenger* remember your e-mail password (unless you do not want students to have access to your new e-mail messages).

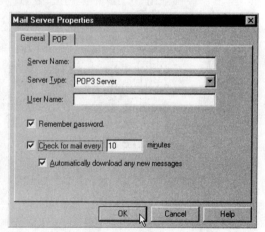

Check the box to have *Messenger* automatically check for new e-mail messages, and set the time interval for checking messages to a specific number of minutes.

Menu Bar *(cont.)*

Click the *Newsgroup Servers* category.

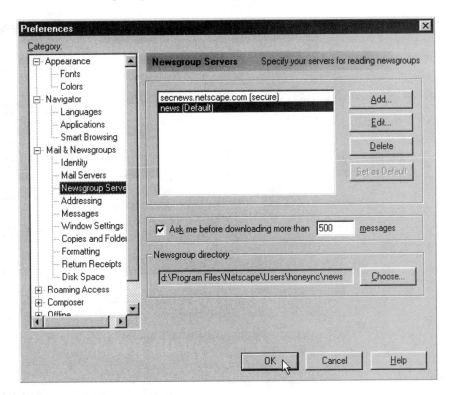

The default (or normal) newsgroup setting is "news." There are many newsgroups about various topics including software and hardware available. This will be discussed more in the *Messenger* section of this book. For now, this is where you would add newsgroup servers.

The option is already checked to ask your permission to download whenever there are more than 500 new messages. You can change that number to a smaller number if you have limited hard drive space. You can also delete that step by clicking the box to remove the check mark beside that option.

Menu Bar *(cont.)*

Click the *Addressing* category.

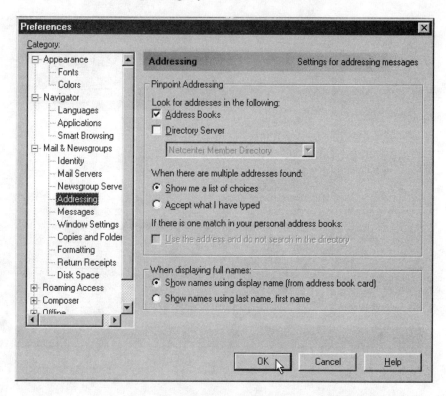

This dialog box lets you set the location of your stored outgoing e-mail addresses. The default is for *Messenger* to search among your local (on your computer) e-mail address books.

Note: If you attempt to send e-mail and your address books are not listed in *Messenger*, you may want to check this preference dialog box to make sure **Address Books** is still checked.

Menu Bar *(cont.)*

Click the ***Messages*** category.

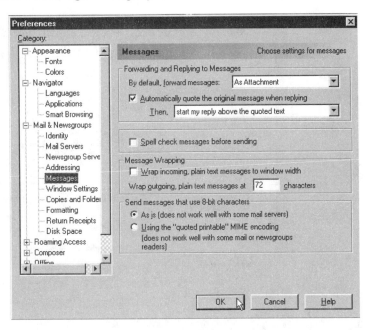

You can set forwarded messages to be sent as attachments or as quoted text. Quoted text will put it in an e-mail message, and then you can also add to the e-mail message.

When replying to a received e-mail message, you can have the original message included in the outgoing e-mail. You can then delete parts of that text and add your own comments before sending your reply. You can select to start your reply above or below the quoted text.

Messenger will spell check your outgoing messages if you select that box.

Note: If you have a project in which your students write e-mail messages to you, you may want to make sure the spell check option is not selected so you can check their spelling in the message.

Menu Bar *(cont.)*

Click the *Window Settings* category.

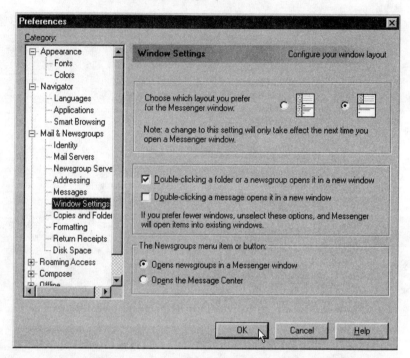

You can use this dialog box to set your preference for how your e-mail and newsgroup message window appears.

You can have a large area for mail and newsgroup boxes. You can select the setting that makes the message box larger. This will make it easier to read incoming messages.

Menu Bar *(cont.)*

Click the ***Copies and Folders*** category.

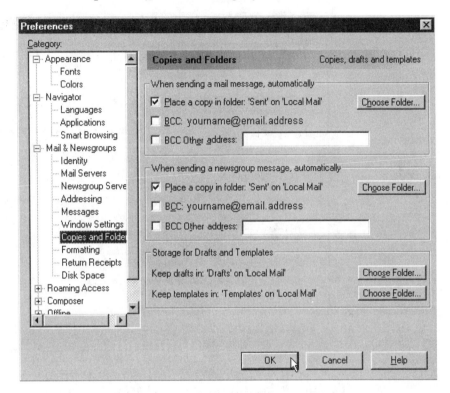

To keep a copy of your outgoing mail messages, select the box to ***Place a copy in folder:***, and choose a folder where you would like to keep these messages.

If you are sending messages from your school e-mail address and would like to keep a copy of the message on your home e-mail, click ***BCC:*** (Blind Carbon Copy) ***yourname@e-mail.address***. Your actual e-mail address will appear here.

If you would like a copy sent to a different e-mail address, click in the ***BCC Other address:*** box and enter the other e-mail address.

These options are also available for newsgroup messages, as well.

Menu Bar *(cont.)*

Click the *Formatting* category.

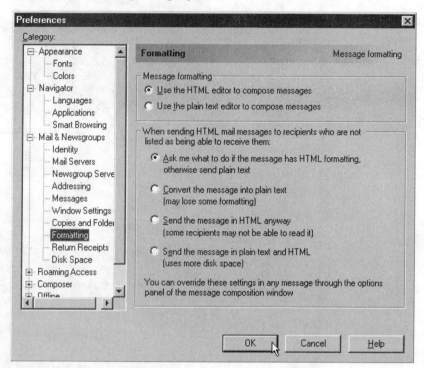

This dialog box allows you to change the way you format outgoing messages.

Most new e-mail software will receive messages as HTML (HyperText Markup Language), similar to a Web page. If you know you will be sending messages to people who cannot read HTML in their e-mail, you may want to change the settings here. You can also override these settings in the individual messages.

Try to be aware of what type of messages your recipients can read. If they cannot read your message, they will not be able to respond to your statements or questions. This is especially important if you have your students sending e-mail messages. You want their messages to reach the students at the destination address.

Menu Bar *(cont.)*

Click the **Return Receipts** category.

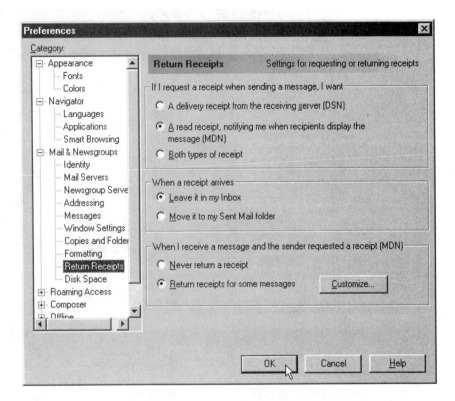

If you are sending important e-mail messages and want to make sure they are received, you can request a return receipt. This dialog box lets you set up how you want those receipts handled.

You can get a receipt to let you know the message has been delivered to the e-mail address.

You can also get a receipt to let you know when the recipient opens that e-mail message.

You can also customize whether you want return receipts sent to other people who request them from you. Click the **Customize** button to set up those preferences.

Menu Bar *(cont.)*

Click the ***Disk Space*** category.

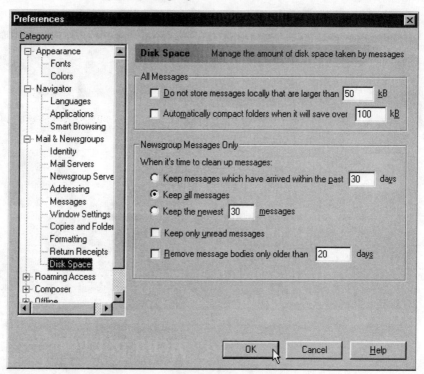

This dialog box allows you to manage your disk space. If you have a lot of hard disk space available, space used to save messages will not have a critical effect. If, however, you have a small disk drive, you may want to manage your usage more closely.

You can tell *Messenger* not to store large e-mail or newsgroup messages. The default is for messages larger than 50 KB (kilobytes), but you can change that message size.

You can also set your newsgroup preferences to keep only current messages or to keep all messages. You can have it delete any messages you have already read or messages that are older than a specified number of days.

Menu Bar *(cont.)*

Click the ***Composer*** category.

This dialog box allows you to set your preferences for composing or editing your own Web pages.

You may want to set *Composer* to automatically save your work periodically. The default setting is to save every 10 minutes.

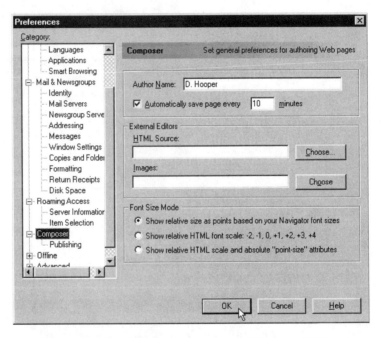

You can use external editing programs to edit your Web page source code and graphic images.

If you have these editing programs available on your computer, click the ***Choose*** button.

Select the editing program from the correct folder on your computer's hard drive.

Menu Bar *(cont.)*

The program launch file will be displayed in this dialog box. When you later use *Composer*, the HTML Source editor will be available from the menu bar.

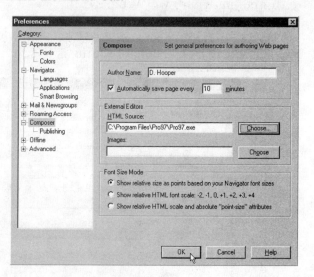

You can follow the same instructions for linking the launch file for your graphic image editing program. It will then be easy to access while using *Composer*.

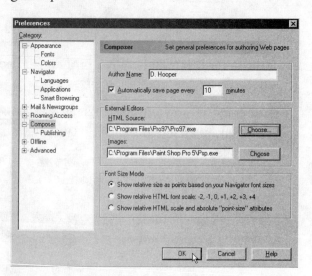

Menu Bar *(cont.)*

Click the ***Publishing*** category.

If you will be publishing your Web pages to an online Web site, you can set these options for *Composer*.

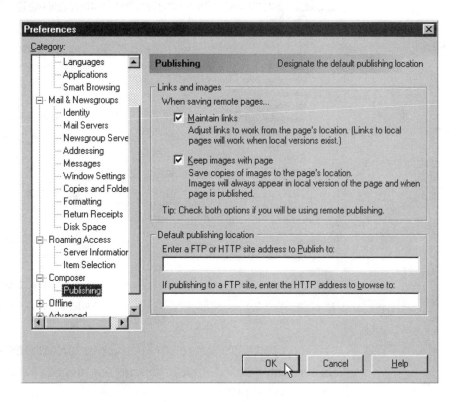

When saving a page to a remote location, you will want to have *Composer* adjust links and images to work at the page's new location. Make sure both of those options have check marks beside them.

If you know the FTP (File Transfer Protocol) or HTTP (HyperText Transfer Protocol) information for your Web site, you can enter it in the blanks, and *Composer* will know where to publish your pages.

Menu Bar *(cont.)*

Click the *Offline* category.

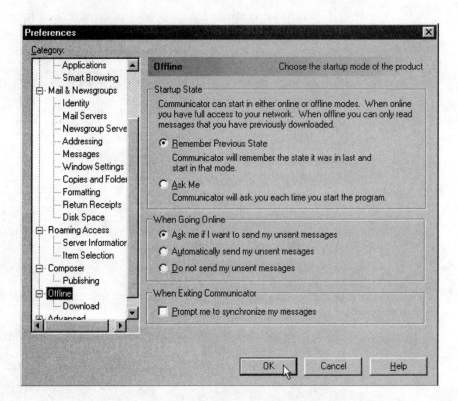

Netscape can be used even if you are not logged on with your Internet service provider. This is offline use.

You can set it to either remember what you were doing the last time you used the program or to ask you every time you start a *Communicator* utility.

You can write messages in *Messenger* while offline and then have it send the messages as soon as you go online. Select whether you want *Messenger* to ask you about sending messages or to automatically send them.

Menu Bar *(cont.)*

Click the ***Download*** category.

This dialog box allows you to set the preferences for newsgroups to which you may subscribe. This will instruct *Messenger* to download messages for your offline use.

You can have *Messenger* download only messages you have not read. You can also specify a length of time, from one week to one year, for *Messenger* to look back for messages.

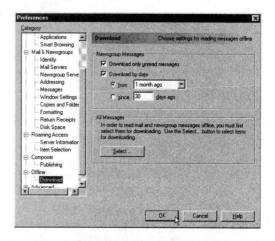

You must select which newsgroups' messages you want to have *Messenger* download.

Click the ***Select*** button.

From the ***Select Items*** dialog box, choose the newsgroups you would like to have downloaded to your computer's hard drive.

Note: Remember that these messages will take up space on your hard drive. If space is limited, you may not want to use this option.

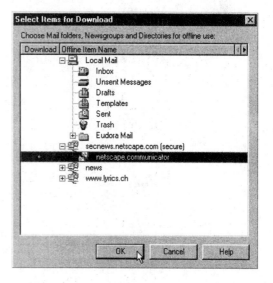

Menu Bar *(cont.)*

Click the *Advanced* category.

Advanced options allow you to indicate how you want *Navigator* to handle Web page functions.

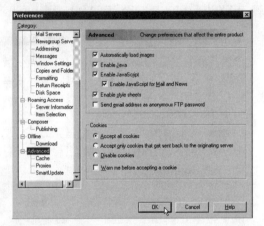

The default is for images to be loaded when you visit a Web page. If your connection is slow, you may want to disable image loading.

Many Web pages have Java coding for activities, animations, and small program applications that are interpreted by *Navigator*. The default is for Java and JavaScript to be enabled. If you are having difficulty loading a Web page, you may want to disable this feature.

If you will be publishing Web pages to an online Web site via FTP technology, click in the square next to *Send e-mail address as anonymous FTP password*. This will allow you to enter FTP sites that require a password for anonymous access.

"Cookies" are entrance tokens that your computer receives when visiting some Web sites or entering information at those sites. If you accept cookies, you will not have to enter that information every time you visit the Web site. Some Web users prefer not to accept that information. If you would rather not, you can click *Disable cookies*.

Menu Bar *(cont.)*

Click the *Cache* category.

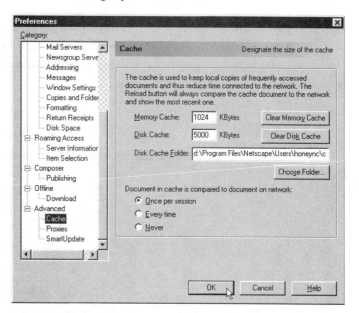

The cache is a place in your computer's memory and on your hard drive where copies of Web pages and graphics you frequently visit are stored. Do not reduce the size of the cache default. You can, however, increase it if you have the memory and hard drive space available. This will reduce the amount of time it takes for those Web pages to load.

If you are having difficulty loading Web pages, you may want to click the *Clear Memory Cache* and *Clear Disk Cache* buttons to manually clear those storage areas.

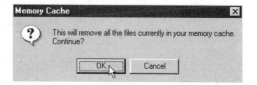

You will see this confirmation box when you click to clear a cache area. To proceed, simply click the *OK* button.

Menu Bar *(cont.)*

Click the ***Proxies*** category.

If you are connected to the Internet from a school or business connection which is behind a firewall (a network protection), you will need to change the settings in this dialog box in order to access Web sites.

Check with your computer technician to find out if you are behind a firewall.

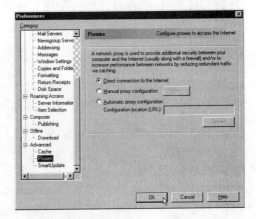

Click the ***SmartUpdate*** category.

The default is for SmartUpdate to be enabled. This allows you to easily access the *Netscape* Netcenter and update your *Netscape Communicator* software package as upgrades are made available.

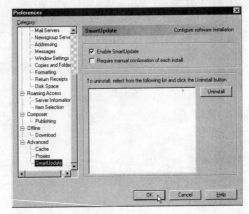

Menu Bar *(cont.)*

View Menu

The View menu on the menu bar allows you to pick what you want to see in your *Navigator* window.

- Click **View**.
- Click **Show**, and all of the tool bars will be listed.

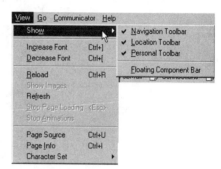

Note: As you and your students learn to use the various *Netscape* components, it is recommended that you leave all of the tool bars visible.

There is a tool bar for all of your *Netscape* components. You can select the option to have it visible on your desktop area.

- Click **View**.
- Click **Show**.
- Click **Floating Component Bar**.

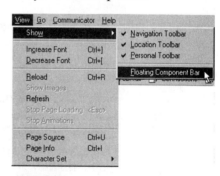

This bar will appear on your desktop area, and you can position it wherever you will find it easily accessible.

If you want to remove it from your desktop, follow the above directions and click to remove the check mark from beside the Floating Component Bar.

Menu Bar *(cont.)*

In order to see what the HTML
coding for a Web page looks
like, choose the Page Source
view.

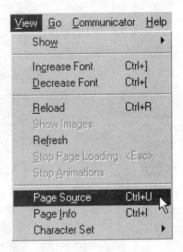

- Click *View*.
- Click *Page Source*.

A new window will open. The coding for the current Web page
(or frame within a Web page) will appear.

```
※ Source of: file:///C|/Internet/Haven/chatters.htm - Netscape

<!doctype html public "-//w3c//dtd html 4.0 transitio
<html>
<head>
    <meta http-equiv="Content-Type" content="text/html
    <meta name="GENERATOR" content="Mozilla/4.5 [en] (
    <title>Favorite Links</title>
</head>
<body text="#34282C" bgcolor="#3BB9FF" link="#151B8D"

<center><img SRC="heron.gif" height=150 width=98></ce

<center>
<h1>
<i>Favorite NetSpots</i></h1></center>

<h3>
```

Looking at the source code for interesting Web pages will give
you and your students ideas about how to create your own pages.

Menu Bar *(cont.)*

Go Menu

As you browse through Web sites, *Navigator* will keep a running list of sites you have visited. If you want to jump back to a previous site, you can use the Go menu options.

- Click *Go*.
- Click the Web page listing that you would like to revisit.

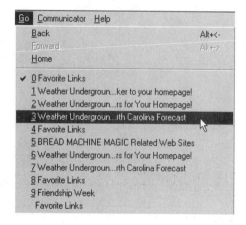

Communicator Menu

The *Communicator* menu is available in all of the components. To launch a component while using a different component, use this option.

- Click *Communicator*.
- Click the component you want to launch.

Menu Bar *(cont.)*

There are several tools available in the *Communicator* menu. You should become familiar with the History file. It will give you an accurate record of where your students have been browsing while using *Navigator*.

- Click **Communicator**.
- Click **Tools**.
- Click **History**.

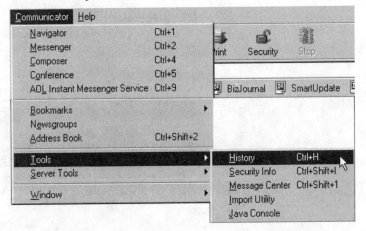

You will see a list of all of the Web sites that have been visited by your computer. You have set the time span in the Preferences section of the Edit menu. You can also clear the History file in the Preferences section of the Edit menu.

To visit a Web site listed in the History file, just double-click the Web page title.

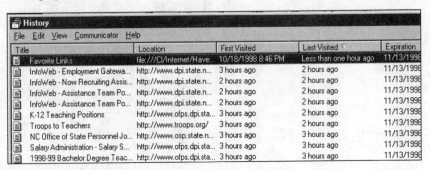

Menu Bar *(cont.)*

Another tool available to you is Security Information. You can check the security level of a Web site you are viewing.

- Click *Communicator*.
- Click *Tools*.
- Click *Security Info*.

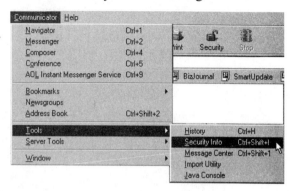

A dialog box similar to this one will allow you to check the security level, password requirements, and other information about the current Web page.

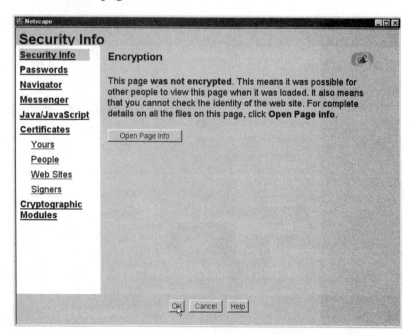

The rest of these tools will be described within other *Communicator* components.

Menu Bar *(cont.)*

Help Menu

In order to find additional information about using *Netscape Communicator* components, you can use the online help file.

- Click *Help*.
- Click *Help Contents*.

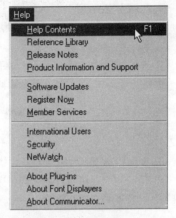

The Help table of contents will appear. You can browse through the topics listed here for additional details about a variety of topics. The Help file is available within all of *Netscape*'s components.

Menu Bar *(cont.)*

From within the Help file, click the ***Index*** button. This will give you a search tool to find information about a specific topic within the *Netscape* Help file.

Key in a keyword or phrase about which you want more information. Click the topic headings as they appear in the list.

Navigating the World Wide Web

Now that you have your *Netscape Communicator* software set up properly, it is time to start traveling around the World Wide Web. The World Wide Web is that part of the Internet that developed when graphical browsers were introduced to computer users.

The work, which began in 1989, centered on the development of the HyperText Transfer Protocol (HTTP). This is a network protocol for requesting and transmitting Web files and documents which both Web servers and browsers of any computer format can understand. By 1993, browser software was released to the public, and the formation of Web sites has grown rapidly since then.

URLs & Hyperlinks

A URL or Uniform Resource Locator references each page on the World Wide Web. This is its Internet address. Once you know an active URL, you can visit that Web page.

Note: Remember that some URLs are "case sensitive." It makes a difference whether that capital letter should be capitalized or not. Punctuation is also crucial. If you key in the URL incorrectly, you will not go to the correct site. You may not go to any Web site at all.

Time to start visiting some Web pages.

If you know a URL, you can key it into the ***Location Box***. The first Web page you will visit is **The Education Haven**.

1. Key this URL into the Location Box in your *Navigator* window:

   http://www.geocities.com/Athens/1573/educate.html

2. Press the ***Enter*** key.

URLs & Hyperlinks *(cont.)*

You should see this Web page in your browser window. It is a listing of educational Web sites that have been organized into subject categories.

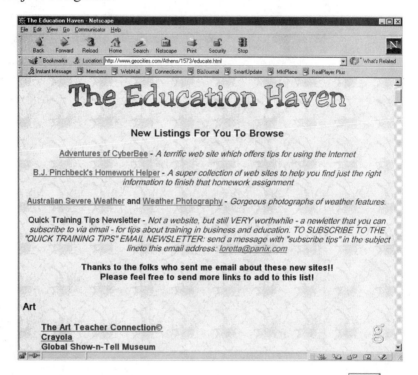

To see more of the list, move the scroll bar on the right-hand side of the Web page up or down. As you move down the list, you will see headings and Web site names.

You should notice that the Web site names are in a different-color text and are underlined. They are links to other Web sites. These are called "hypertext links" or "hyperlinks." When you use your mouse to click a hyperlink, your browser will travel to that Web page.

URLs & Hyperlinks *(cont.)*

As you scroll down the list, you will see the various categories of Web sites.

Scroll down to the Stories section of the Language Arts category.

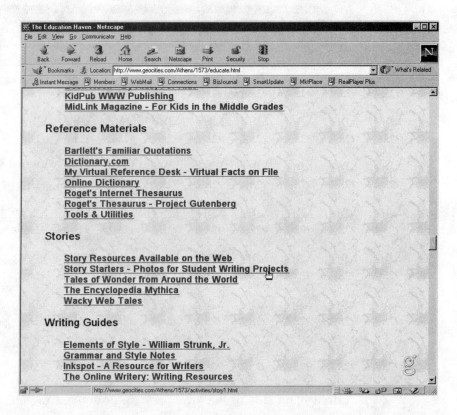

Move your mouse so it is over the hyperlink:

Story Starters—Photos for Student Writing Projects

You will notice that your cursor changes from the arrow shape to the shape of a small hand. Any time you see the hand shape, your cursor is resting over a hyperlink.

With your cursor over the hyperlink, click once with your left mouse button.

URLs & Hyperlinks *(cont.)*

The link will take you to a second Web page containing the **Story Starters**. This Web page contains photographs that can be used to spark your students' imaginations when they have to create stories.

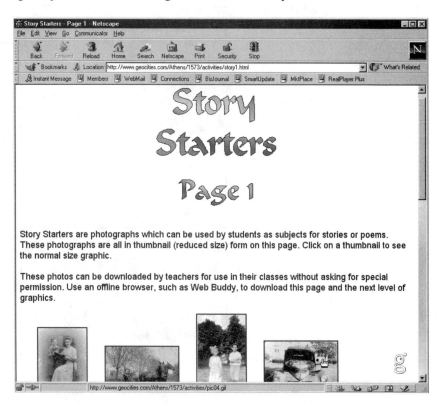

The small photographs on the page are called "thumbnails." They are also hyperlinks. If you move your cursor over them, you will notice it changes to the small hand cursor. You should notice also that they have a border around them. This is much like the underlining of text hyperlinks. It is a clue that the graphic is a link to another Web page.

Move your mouse over the photograph of the old car. Use your left mouse button to click the photograph.

URLs & Hyperlinks *(cont.)*

You should see a larger copy of the photograph. Quite often, Web sites will have larger copies of photographs and other graphics available if you click the thumbnail. Thumbnails are quicker for your browser to open.

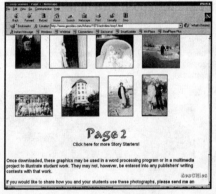

Sometimes, there will not be a link for you to click to get back to the previous Web page. Click the **Back** button on the navigation tool bar to retrace your path.

If you scroll further down on the Web page, you will see a graphic that says Page 2. It does not have a border around it, but if you move your mouse over it, you will see that your cursor changes to the small hand. This is also a hyperlink that uses a graphic. If you click the **Page 2** hyperlink, you will go to another Web page of photographs.

URLs & Hyperlinks *(cont.)*

Try visiting **B. J. Pinchbeck's Homework Helper** Web site. A student and his father created it. They wanted to organize a group of Web sites for students to use to help them find answers to homework problems. They have also included some wonderful resource Web sites for teachers.

1. Key this URL into the Location Box:

   http://tristate.pgh.net/~pinch13/

2. Press the ***Enter*** key.

This Web page is divided into sections called "frames." There is an index list of hyperlinks in the frame on the left and other informative Web pages on the right.

3. Click the hyperlink for ***Computers and the Internet***.

URLs & Hyperlinks *(cont.)*

Once you have clicked the hyperlink, you should see the following Web page. It is a list of other Web pages about Computer Science and the Internet. Sites like Education Haven and B. J. Pinchbeck's Homework Helper will save you time while searching for related Web sites. They are index sites where others share their hours of searching the World Wide Web.

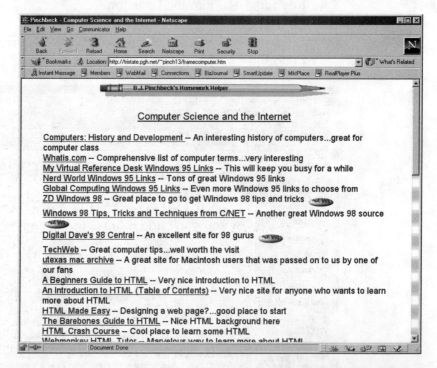

Another way for you to find related Web sites is to click the ***What's Related*** drop-down menu to the right of the Location Box. *Netscape* will give you a list of sites that are similar to the Web site you are visiting. You can then click one of those links and see a list of other Web sites.

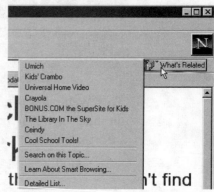

URLs & Hyperlinks *(cont.)*

The Discovery Channel has an excellent Web site with content about various topics, classroom activities, and teacher resources, which complements their programming.

1. Key this URL into the Location Box:

   http://discoveryschool.com/

2. Press the ***Enter*** key.

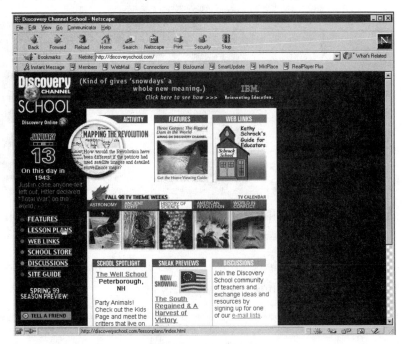

You should see this Web page. It is the beginning or home page for Discovery Channel School. There are some hypertext links and some thumbnail photographs you can use to travel through the Web site. There are also buttons on the left-hand side of the Web page. Buttons are another way for Webmasters (people who design Web pages) to lead you to other Web pages.

1. Move your cursor over ***LESSON PLANS***.

2. Click that button.

URLs & Hyperlinks *(cont.)*

You should now be at the Discovery School Lesson Plans Web page. There are many subject areas listed. Each of those subjects is also a hyperlink.

1. Move your cursor to *LITERATURE*.
2. Click that hyperlink.

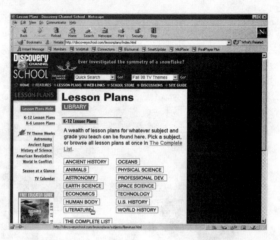

You will see a list of lesson plans related to various works of literature.

3. Move your cursor to ***Tales from the Brothers Grimm***.
4. Click that hyperlink.

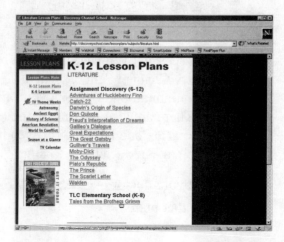

URLs & Hyperlinks *(cont.)*

This is an example of what you will find in the lesson plan section. Each lesson plan consists of several parts. You will need to click each hyperlink to read the rest of this lesson.

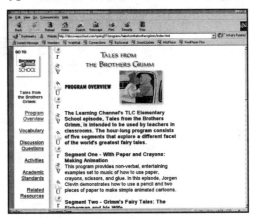

5. Use your **Back** button to return to the **Discovery School** home page.

6. Scroll to the bottom of this Web page. You will see a section called **Search Our Resources**, which is a "search engine" for this Web site. There are many Web pages at this site, and this is another way for you to find what you need.

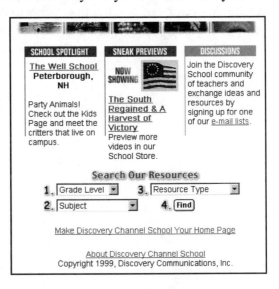

URLs & Hyperlinks *(cont.)*

You can click the arrows to select grade levels and topics to meet your criteria.

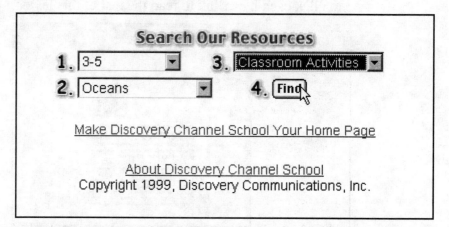

Try this:

1. Choose grade levels 3–5.
2. Choose the topic Oceans.
3. Choose Classroom Activities.
4. Click the *Find* button.

Once you click the *Find* button, the search program at this Web site will search through the database of information and send the results back to you on another Web page.

URLs & Hyperlinks *(cont.)*

This search shows two resources found. Each site is listed as a hyperlink with a description of what you will find on that Web page.

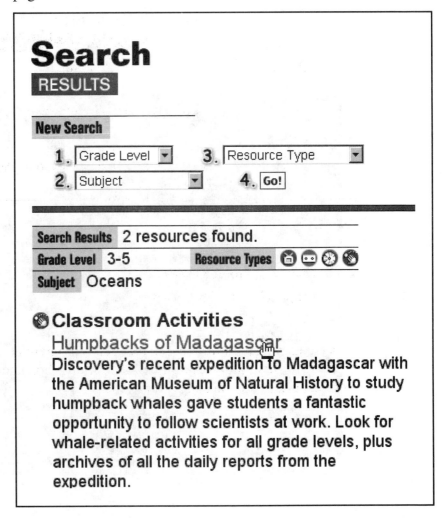

5. Click the hyperlink for ***Humpbacks of Madagascar*** to visit that Web page.

URLs & Hyperlinks *(cont.)*

Navigator should take you to this page about the humpback whales.

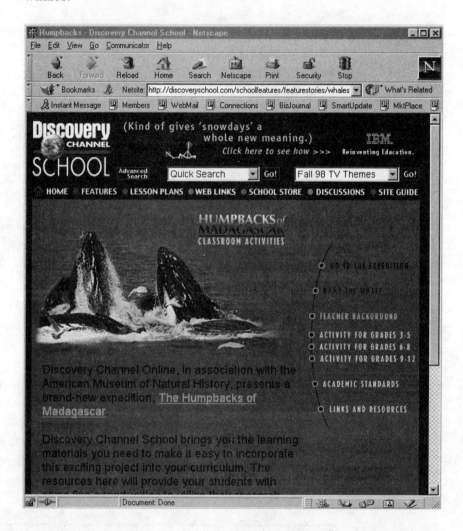

From this page, you can click the ***Teacher Background***, ***Activity***, and ***Links and Resources*** links.

URLs & Hyperlinks *(cont.)*

Use the ***Back*** button on the tool bar to go back to the home page of the **Discovery School** Web site, and click the graphic hyperlink to **Kathy Schrock's Guide for Educators**.

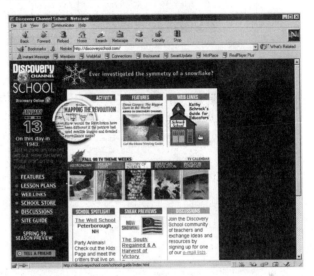

This is another Web site that a teacher should not be without in his or her list of resources. It is another list of educational Web sites that you can use with your classes.

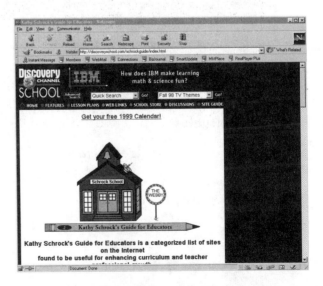

URLs & Hyperlinks *(cont.)*

To go directly to this Web page, key the following URL into the Location Box:

http://discoveryschool.com/schrockguide/index.html

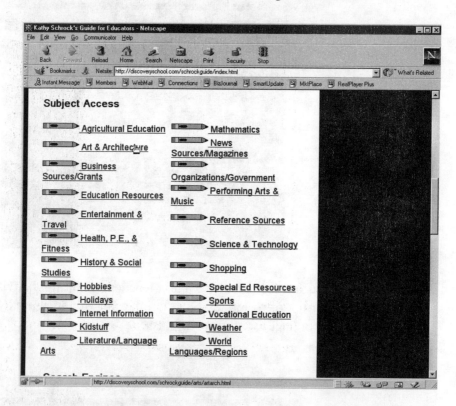

As you scroll down this Web page, you will see various categories of educational Web sites. These are hyperlinks that will take you to the subject lists.

1. Click the ***Art & Architecture*** link.

URLs & Hyperlinks *(cont.)*

Each of the Web sites listed in this guide has a brief explanation written about it. You can click the hyperlinks to visit the listed Web sites.

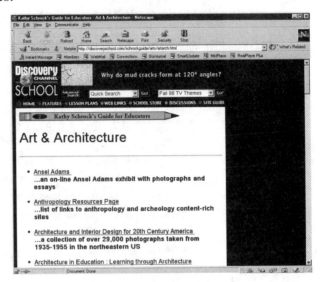

Use the ***Back*** button to return to the index page of the guide. Here you will find teacher resources, such as training guides for teachers and slide shows that have been used as training materials.

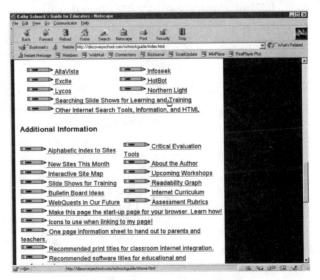

URLs & Hyperlinks *(cont.)*

2. Click the ***Searching Slide Shows for Learning and Training*** link.

3. To view a sample slide show, click ***Slide Show: How to Find It & What to Do With It When You Do.***

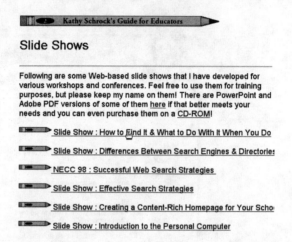

As you can see with this page, not everything on a Web page is hypertext formatting. There are many programs that allow you to publish your presentations online.

Follow the hyperlinks to move through this slide show.

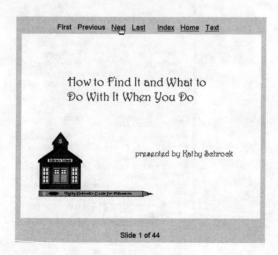

URLs & Hyperlinks *(cont.)*

You can use these slide shows as classroom materials, teacher-training modules, or simply as personal training resources.

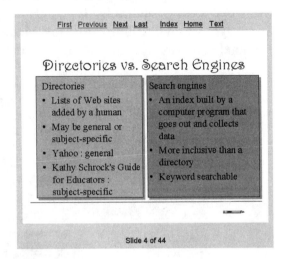

This particular slide show teaches you how to find information on the World Wide Web.

There are tips on how to successfully search for information. It also gives you suggestions for using some of that information once you have found it.

URLs & Hyperlinks *(cont.)*

Another site for you and your students to visit is **MidLink Magazine**. This is a digital magazine created for kids, by kids. First created by students at Ligon GT Magnet Middle School in Raleigh, North Carolina, **MidLink Magazine** has grown into a digital magazine for students all over the world.

1. Key this URL into the Location Box:

   http://longwood.cs.ucf.edu/~MidLink/

2. Press the *Enter* key.

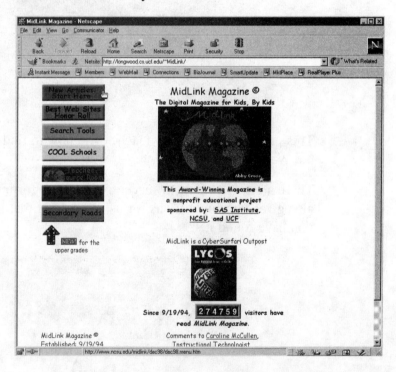

This will take you to the current issue of **MidLink Magazine**. You will see several hypertext links that will lead you to information about the project's sponsors. You will find the graphic hyperlinks on the left-hand side of the Web page.

3. Click the *New Articles: Start Here* button.

URLs & Hyperlinks *(cont.)*

One of this issue's projects is called Monu-MENTAL. The project was designed for other schools to send in their results and become part of the process of sharing information via the Internet.

4. Click ***Monu-MENTAL*** to see some of the projects already online.

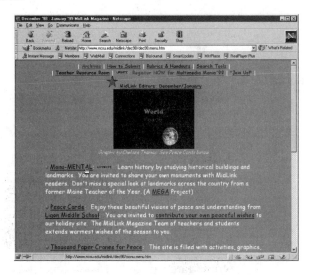

5. Click ***Durant Road Middle School***'s project to see how they shared the governor's mansion with the world.

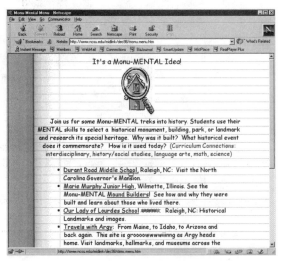

URLs & Hyperlinks *(cont.)*

6. Click the hyperlink, ***Click here to See Slides***, to visit their project.

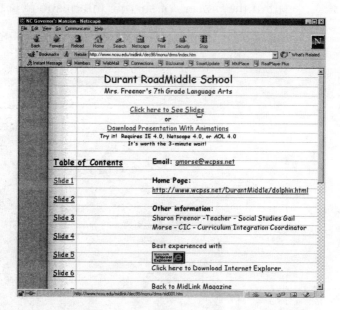

7. To navigate through this slide show, click the buttons.

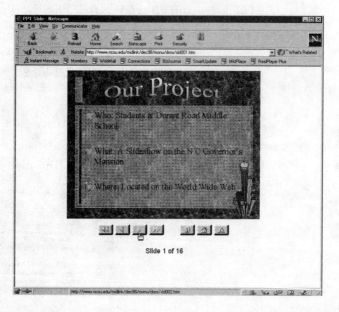

URLs & Hyperlinks *(cont.)*

To visit another Web site created for educators and students:

1. Key this URL into the Location Box:

   http://www.gsn.org/index.html

2. Press the *Enter* key.

The Global Schoolhouse began in 1984 with the FrEdMail (Free Educational) Network. This was a program in which students from various locations could participate in e-mail (electronic mail) projects with each other.

Today there is a wide variety of activities which you and your students can join. A quick way to see this assortment is to go to the **Site At A Glance** Web page.

URLs & Hyperlinks *(cont.)*

3. Click the *Site At A Glance* button on the left-hand side of the Web page.

You will see this index page which gives you many ways to find information available on the Web site.

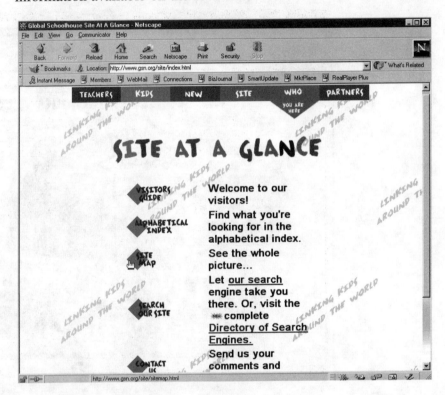

4. Click the *Site Map* hyperlink.

This will take you to an easy-to-view map of all of the topics covered in this Web site.

URLs & Hyperlinks *(cont.)*

This Web page shows various topics that are divided into groups. Although the text is not a different color and is not underlined, each title is a hyperlink to a Web page. As you move your cursor over the text, you will notice the small hand appear.

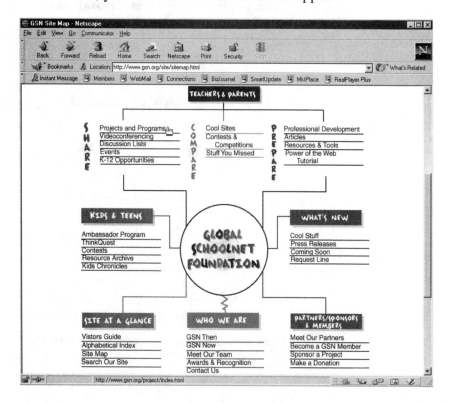

There are sections about sharing information, preparing to use the Internet, new activities or announcements, information about the Global SchoolNet Foundation, and partnerships with other companies and organizations.

5. Click ***Projects and Programs***.

This link will take you to a list of the current projects available for your classes to join.

URLs & Hyperlinks *(cont.)*

6. Click the *GeoGame* hyperlink to see one of the activities. The GeoGame started as an e-mail project, but now has a "Web" format.

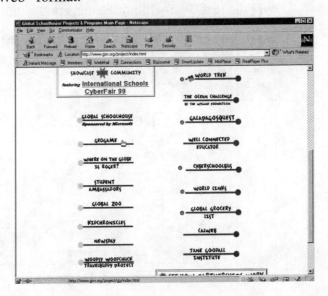

7. Click the *Web GeoGame* hyperlink to see how this game has changed to use the World Wide Web interface.

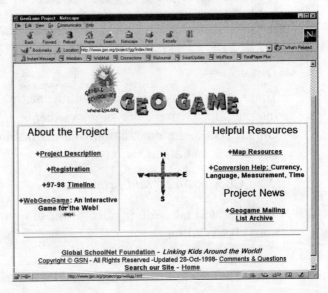

URLs & Hyperlinks *(cont.)*

You can click the description hyperlink to read about how to play the WebGeoGame.

8. Click *Play a Game* to jump right in.

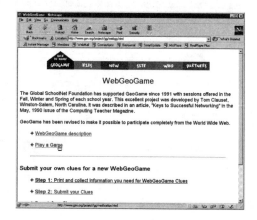

You will be asked to sign in to participate. You will need to fill in your real name and your e-mail address.

9. When you are ready to participate, fill in this information.

10. Then click the *Search* button.

The Global Schoolhouse keeps a database of everyone who participates in these projects. This is to safeguard you and your students from people who do not participate properly.

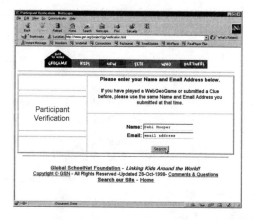

URLs & Hyperlinks *(cont.)*

Once the Web site recognizes you as a registered participant, you can either choose to play a game or submit your own clues. Take a look at some sets of clues before you enter any of your own.

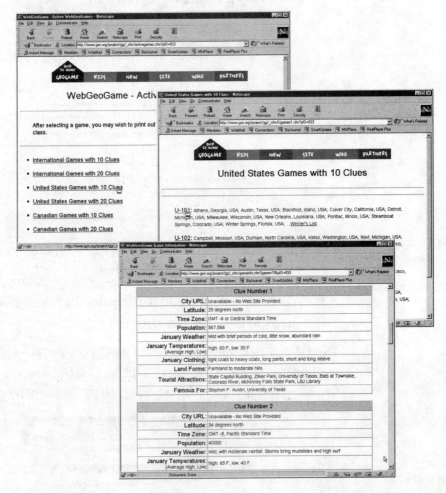

Click the hypertext links to make choices about which type of game you want your students to play. You will then see a set of clues to locations in the United States, Canada, or the world. Your students can solve these puzzles, and you can submit their responses. This is a super activity, even if you are not participating online.

URLs & Hyperlinks *(cont.)*

Another type of hyperlink site map is an Image Map.

1. Key this URL into your Location Box.

   http://www.ars.usda.gov/is/kids/

2. Press the ***Enter*** key.

The United States Department of Agriculture has a **Sci4Kids** Web site full of activities to help children learn about scientists and agriculture.

When you see this Web site's home page, you do not see any hyperlinks. Instead of underlined text, buttons, or individual graphics to click, you see one big graphic image that is divided into "invisible" hyperlinks.

Try this:

3. Click the silly-faced ***Venus Flytrap*** under the magnifying glass.

URLs & Hyperlinks *(cont.)*

As the silly face on that ***Venus Flytrap*** might have suggested, this hyperlink takes you to the **Weird Science** Web page.

This Web page supplies scientific answers to weird questions asked by kids.

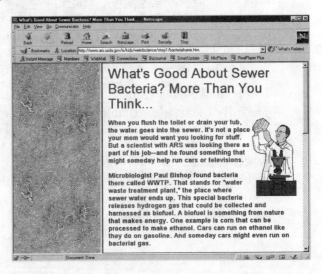

4. Click the question and follow that hyperlink to the answer Web page.

URLs & Hyperlinks *(cont.)*

At the main menu, selecting the scientist with the light bulb head hyperlink allows your students to find out information about various types of scientists.

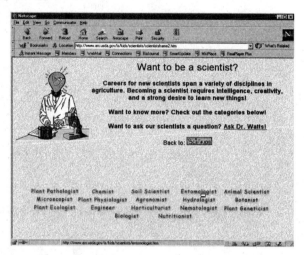

This is also a Web page that is divided into frames. There is a frame across the top in addition to the one across the bottom of each page. As your students read through the information about the scientists, they do not have to return to the starting page to make another selection.

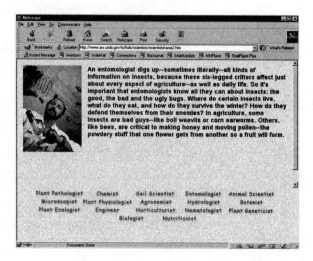

URLs & Hyperlinks *(cont.)*

Another site with an example of an Image Map is the **National Weather Service** Web site.

1. Key this URL into the Location Box.

   http://www.nws.noaa.gov/

2. Press the **Enter** key.

3. Click the graphic of the United States to go to a Web page with a "clickable" map of the states.

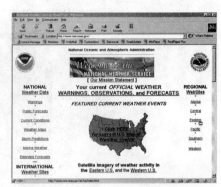

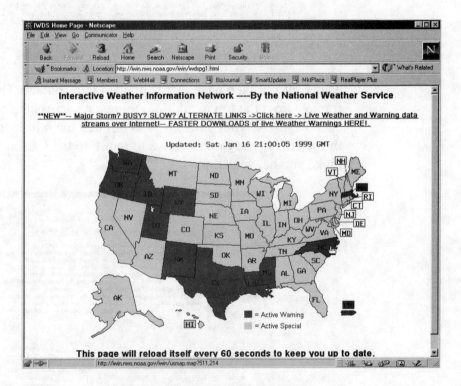

To find current weather information about your state, click the state on the image map.

URLs & Hyperlinks *(cont.)*

Each state also has an image map showing cities that have local weather reports available.

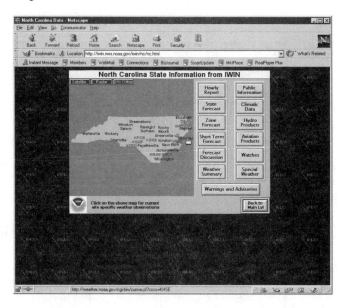

4. Click a city name to see the report Web page.

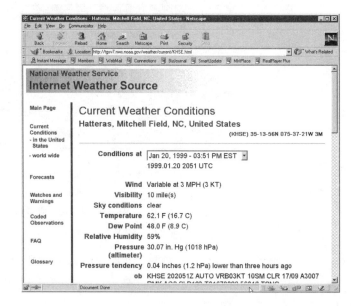

URLs & Hyperlinks *(cont.)*

What will happen when you enter an incorrect URL, or the hyperlink you click is incorrect, or the Web page no longer exists? You will see one of a variety of error messages.

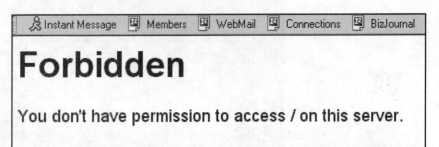

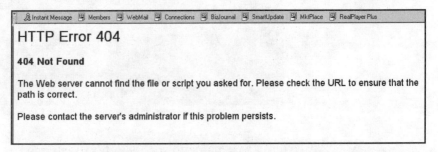

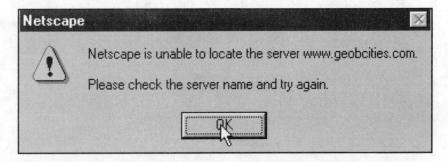

Do not let the language used in the error message scare you. It is not personal. These are stock messages that are delivered by a network computer to let you know the Web page URL you have tried to access does not exist.

Check your spelling, capitalization, and punctuation first. If those are all correct, then perhaps the Web page no longer exists.

Bookmarks

When you find Web sites that you do not want to lose, you can create a bookmark for an easy link back to that site. *Navigator* also allows you to organize your bookmarks into folders that you create.

To visit the **White House** Web site:

1. Key this URL into the Location Box.

   http://www.whitehouse.gov

2. Press the *Enter* key.

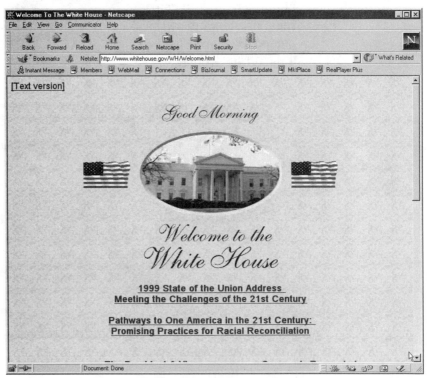

Notice that the URL in your Location Box changes to:

   http://www.whitehouse.gov/WH/Welcome.html

The **White House** computer changes this automatically as it leads you to the welcome Web page.

Bookmarks *(cont.)*

You may find it difficult to remember different URLs. By creating a bookmark you will not have to remember them or write them down.

There are several ways to create your bookmark file.

1. Click the **Bookmarks** button.

2. Click **Add Bookmark**.

3. Click the **Bookmarks** button again. You can see a new bookmark named **Welcome To The White House**.

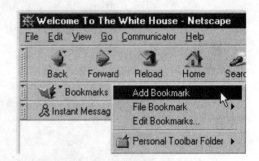

You have just created your first bookmark.

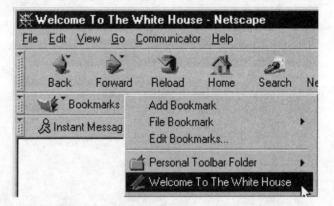

If you think about this method for a minute, you will realize that if you start adding a bookmark for all of the interesting Web sites that you find, you could rapidly collect a long list.

In order to keep your bookmark file organized, *Navigator* allows you to create folders in which to group your bookmarks in some kind of order. One folder was already created as soon as you installed *Netscape*, the Personal Toolbar Folder. It has the bookmarks in it that represent the buttons on the Personal Toolbar in your *Navigator* window.

Bookmarks *(cont.)*

You will need to create bookmark folders before you can put bookmarks into them.

4. Click the **Bookmarks** button.

5. Click *Edit Bookmarks*.

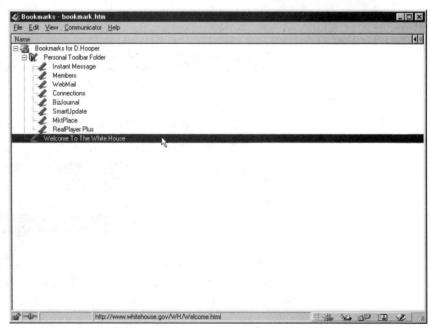

The bookmark editing utility will appear. This is where you create folders and edit or delete bookmarks. You should be able to see the bookmark for **The White House** at the bottom of the list.

Bookmarks *(cont.)*

6. Click *File*.
7. Click *New Folder*.

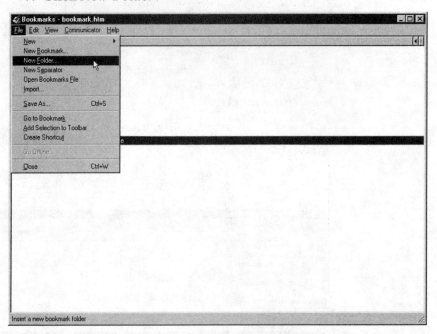

This dialog box will appear.

8. Key School into the *Name*: box.

9. Click the *OK* button.

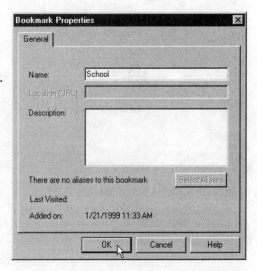

Bookmarks *(cont.)*

10. Click *File*, and *Close* to close the editing utility.

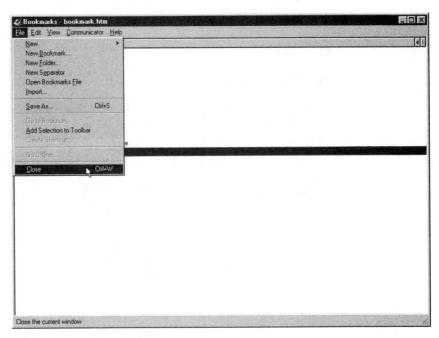

Now you have a folder in which to file bookmarks.

11. Click *Bookmarks*.

12. Click *File Bookmarks*.

13. Continue to move your mouse cursor and select *School*.

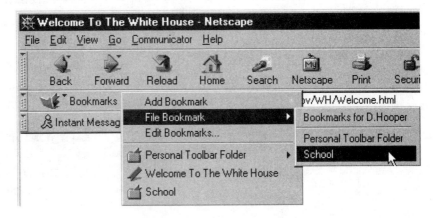

Bookmarks *(cont.)*

Now take a look at your new bookmark list.

14. Click *Bookmarks*.
15. Click the *School* folder.

You should see your new bookmark in the School folder.

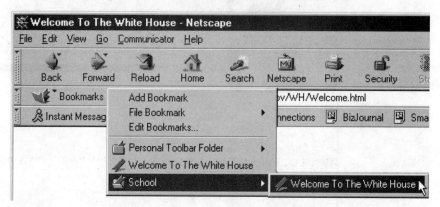

In your classroom, you can make a bookmark folder for each student or team of students using the computer. As they find Web sites that interest them, they can file the bookmarks into their folders.

To delete the original bookmark for **The White House**:

1. Click *Bookmarks*.
2. Click *Edit Bookmarks* to open the editing utility.

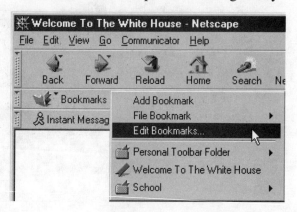

Bookmarks *(cont.)*

3. Click the bookmark for **The White House** once to highlight it.

4. Right-click (click with your right mouse button) the bookmark to open the drop-down menu.

5. Click *Delete Bookmark*. You have now successfully deleted that bookmark from your list.

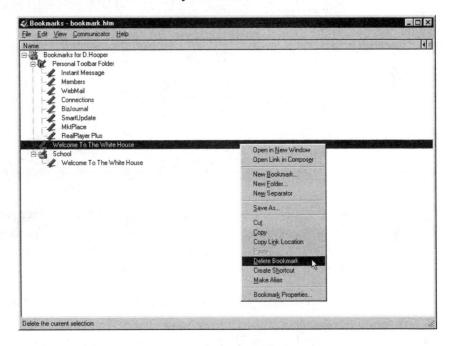

6. Click *Bookmarks* to check your list.

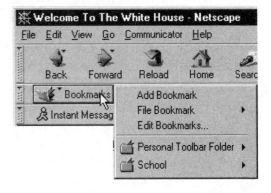

You should see that the single entry for **The White House** is gone now.

Bookmarks *(cont.)*

Continue to add bookmarks to your folders as you find sites you want to remember. Once you have those favorite sites bookmarked, it is easy to go back to visit them.

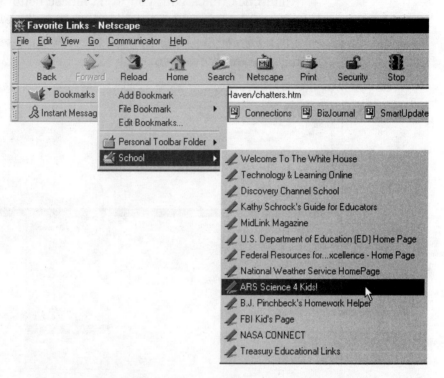

1. Click the ***Bookmarks*** icon.
2. Click the ***School*** folder. You will see a list of all of the sites you have bookmarked.
3. Slide your cursor over to the list of bookmarks and select the Web site you want to visit.
4. Click the Web site in the list. *Navigator* will take you to that Web site.

Bookmarks *(cont.)*

If you work at home and collect a number of bookmarks that you would like to use at school, you can save your bookmark file to a disk and copy it to your school computer.

1. Click **Bookmarks**.

2. Click **Edit Bookmarks** to open the bookmark editing utility.

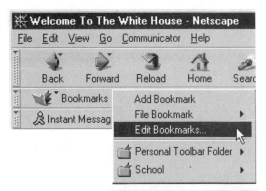

3. Click **File** in the bookmark editing utility.

4. Click **Save As** on the drop-down menu.

5. Select the A: drive if you are planning to take the file to another computer.

6. Click the **Save** button.

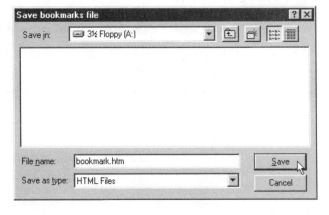

Bookmarks *(cont.)*

7. Insert the disk into the other computer.

8. Open *Netscape Navigator*.

9. Click *File*.

10. Click *Open Page*.

11. Click the *Choose File* button on the *Open Page* dialog box.

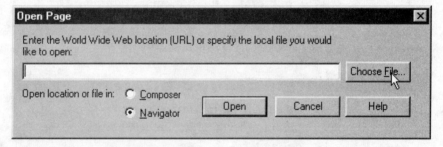

12. Locate the bookmark.htm file on the disk in the A: drive.

13. Click the *Open* button.

Bookmarks *(cont.)*

You will see *A:\bookmark.htm* appear in the blank. If you know the name of your file, you can select it by simply keying in the location and name without browsing for the file.

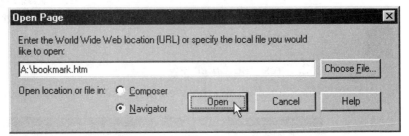

Now that the file location and name are in the blank, click the ***Open*** button.

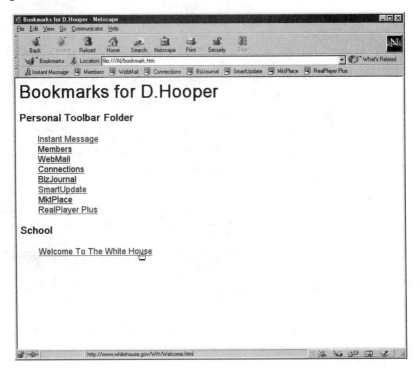

The bookmark file opens in your *Navigator* window as a Web page with hypertext links. To go to one of the links listed, simply click it as you would a hyperlink on any Web page.

Printing Web Pages

In this section, you will learn how to print Web pages on paper.

You can use **The White House** Web site in this example.

1. Key this URL into the Location Box in *Navigator*:
   http://www.whitehouse.gov

2. Press the ***Enter*** key.

3. Scroll down the Web page until you see these menu choices.

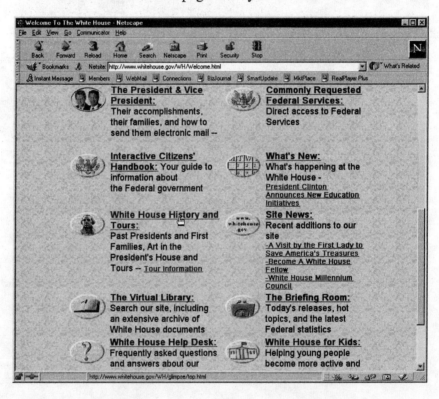

4. Click the ***White House History and Tours***: link.

Printing Web Pages *(cont.)*

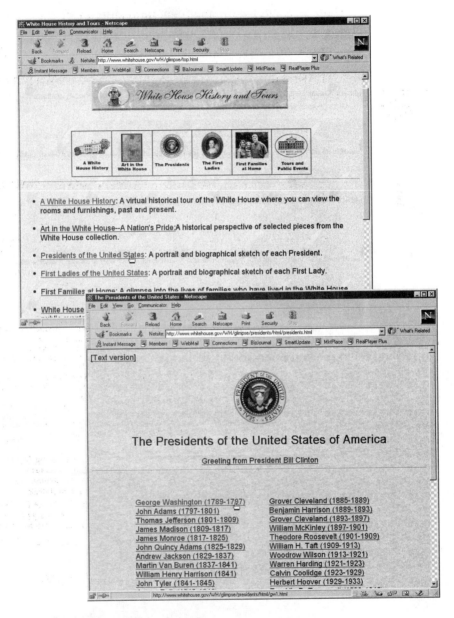

5. Click *Presidents of the United States*.
6. Select *George Washington*.

Printing Web Pages *(cont.)*

There is a Web page about each president. This can be useful information for your social studies class, or it can be used as a template design for a project about mathematicians, scientists, or authors.

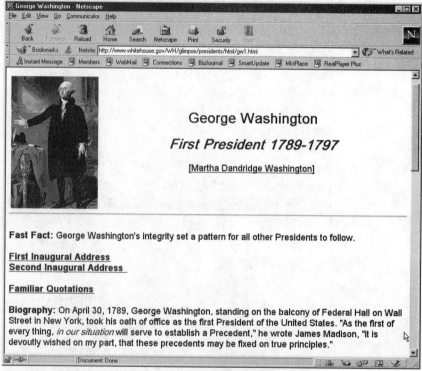

Before printing, you will need to check your page setup.

7. Click *File*.

8. Click *Page Setup*.

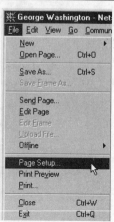

Printing Web Pages *(cont.)*

9. Make sure the page is set the way you want it to print.

10. Click the **OK** button to confirm the setup.

This page is set for half-inch margins all around the page. It will print the Web page document title and URL in the header of the page. In the footer, it will print the page number, total number of pages, and the date you printed the page.

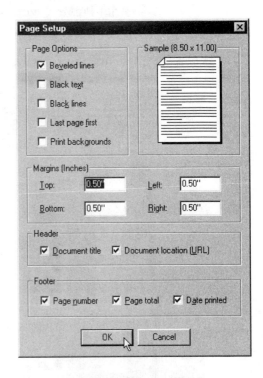

11. Click **File**.

12. Click **Print Preview** to see how your page will look once you print it.

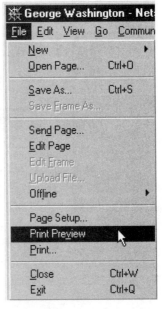

Printing Web Pages *(cont.)*

The Print Preview window will show you your page as it will look when you print it.

13. Click the ***Next Page*** button to view additional pages.

14. Click the ***Close*** button to return to the *Navigator* window.

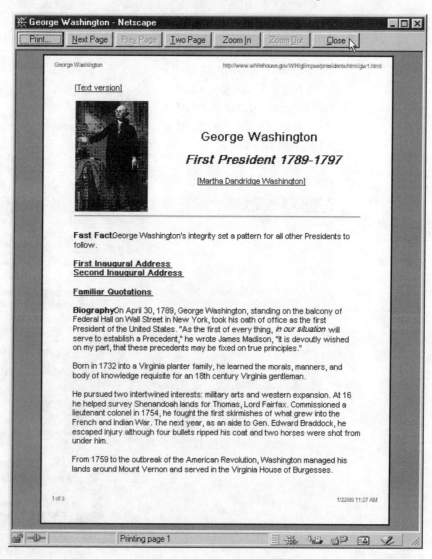

Printing Web Pages *(cont.)*

15. Click *File* and *Print* when you are ready to print the Web pages.

16. Instead of selecting *File* and *Print*, you could just click the *Print* button on your tool bar.

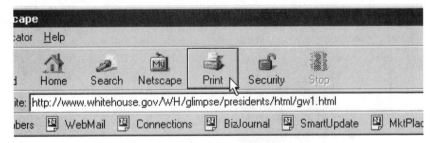

17. When the printer dialog box appears, check your settings for number of copies, etc., and click the *OK* button.

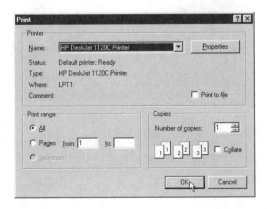

Saving Web Pages

There are many reasons to save a Web page. You can use it as a template file for creating a page of your own. You can print it to share with your students. Or you may simply want to use the Web page with an overhead projector system as part of a lesson.

There are several ways to save a Web page. If you only need to save the text on the page, you can use these simple instructions.

Practice with the same Web page about George Washington.

1. Key this URL into the Location Box.

http://www.whitehouse.gov/WH/glimpse/presidents/html/gw1.html

2. Press the **Enter** key.

You should see this Web page about George Washington.

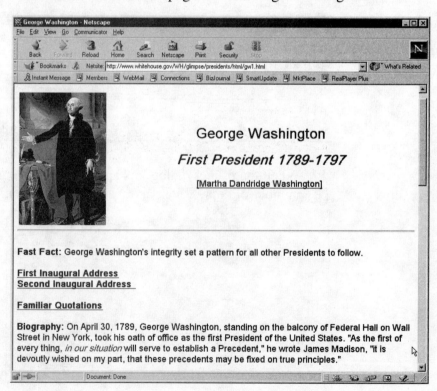

Saving Web Pages *(cont.)*

3. Click *File*.

4. Click *Save As*.

5. In the *Save As* dialog box, select a disk or folder location.

6. Click the *Save* button.

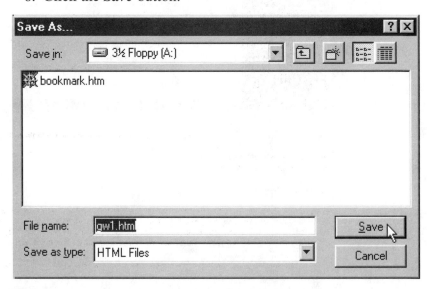

Saving Web Pages *(cont.)*

To view a saved Web page, you will use the Open Page option in the File drop-down menu.

7. Click **File**.

8. Click **Open Page**.

9. Click the **Choose File** button to browse and find the file you want to open.

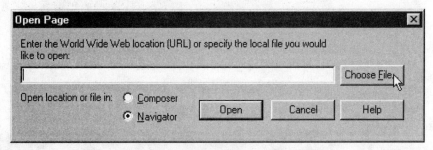

10. Select the file you want to open.

11. Click the **Open** button.

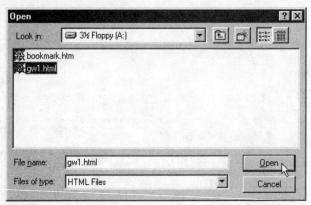

Saving Web Pages *(cont.)*

12. Click the **Open** button in the **Open Page** dialog box.

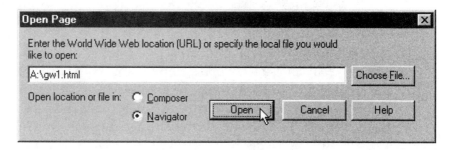

The **George Washington** Web page should look like the following page. You did save all of the text and HTML formatting, but you did not save and retrieve any of the graphics.

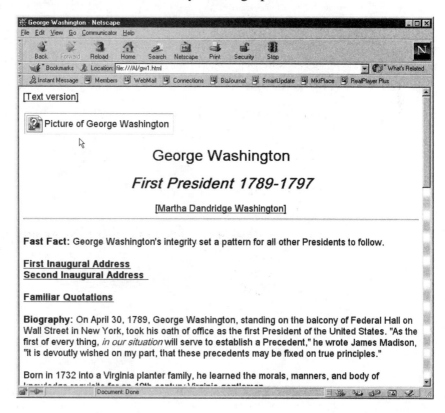

Saving Web Pages *(cont.)*

If you want the graphics to appear also, there are several ways to save the Web page. You can use an offline browser program such as *Web Buddy* to retrieve the entire page and all of the associated files.

You can use *Netscape*'s editing process to retrieve the graphics along with the Web page. It will rewrite the HTML to show that the graphic is in the same folder as the Web page. This is important if the original Web page refers to graphics that are in a different folder or directory.

Start with the **George Washington** Web page again at this URL:

http://www.whitehouse.gov/WH/glimpse/presidents/html/gw1.html

Once you have the Web page open, you can edit the page.

1. Click *File*.
2. Click *Edit* Page.

This will open another *Netscape* window. You should see a *Composer* window open with the **George Washington** Web page in it.

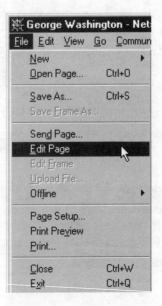

Saving Web Pages *(cont.)*

Notice that you have a new window and the Title Bar says *Netscape Composer*.

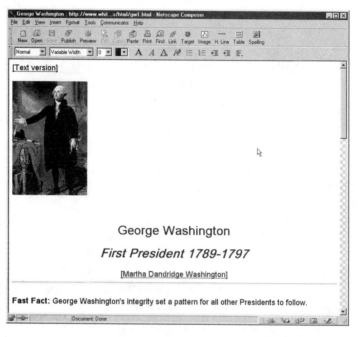

We will cover creating Web pages later in this book. For now, we are using the Composer utility to save the Web page and graphics for later viewing.

3. In the *Composer* window, click *File*.

4. Click *Save As*.

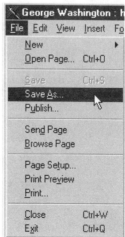

Saving Web Pages *(cont.)*

5. In the *Save As* dialog box, select a location in which to save the Web page file and the associated graphics.

6. Click the *Save* button.

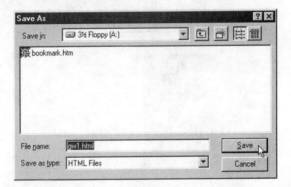

When you save the file this time, you will see a dialog box telling you which graphics are being saved to the folder.

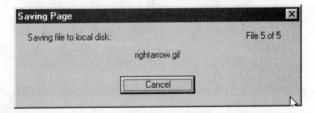

You now want to close the *Composer* window without exiting *Netscape*.

7. Click *File*.

8. Click *Close* (not Exit).

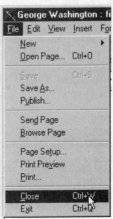

Saving Web Pages *(cont.)*

9. To see which files have been saved to the folder or disk, select *Open Page* from the *File* menu.

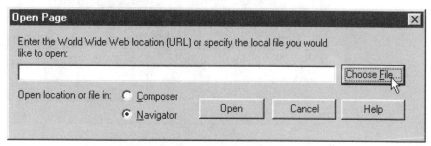

10. Click the *Choose File* button on the *Open Page* dialog box.

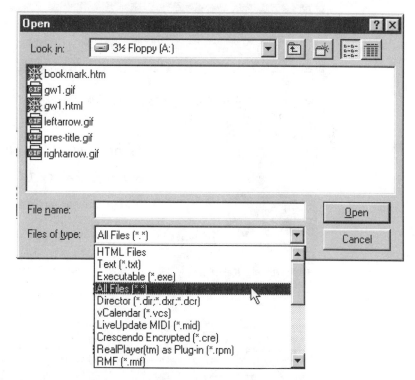

11. Select *All Files* from the *Files of type* name drop-down menu. This will show you all of the files that were saved. You should see the "html" file and some "gif" graphic files, as well.

Saving Web Pages *(cont.)*

12. Select the *gw1.html* file and click **Open**.

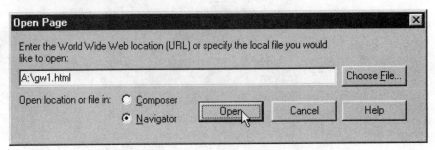

13. Click the **Open** button on the **Open Page** dialog box.

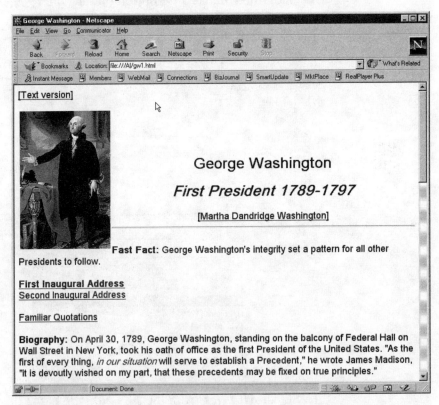

You should now have the complete Web page and graphics in your *Navigator* window instead of just the text.

Saving Files from Web Pages

There will be times when you find a photograph or graphic image that you or your students would like to include in a multimedia presentation or word-processed document.

The first thing you need to do before saving the image is to find out if you are allowed to download it from the Web page. Many Webmasters will be happy for you to use their images and information in school projects or student activities. Unless there is a disclaimer on the Web site or the site is public information, you should ask permission.

Once you know you can download the image, there are a few simple steps you can follow.

You can use some images from the **Earth From Space** Web site for this activity. NASA allows use of their photographs for any educational project.

1. Key this URL into the Location Box and press the **Enter** key.

   http://earth.jsc.nasa.gov/

2. Click the **Clickable Map** hyperlink.

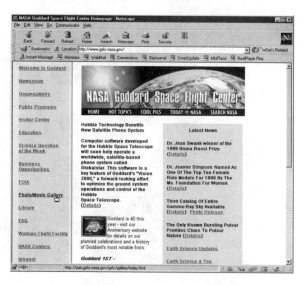

Saving Files from Web Pages *(cont.)*

The photograph gallery is divided into major topics.

3. Click the ***Hurricanes and Weather*** button in the lower left corner.

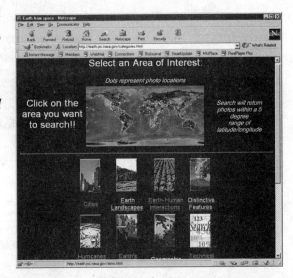

4. From the search menu, scroll down and select ***Hurricanes***.

5. Click the ***Start Search*** button.

You may have to wait a few minutes for the graphics and information to load when you make choices at this Web site. Some topics have more possible graphics than others do.

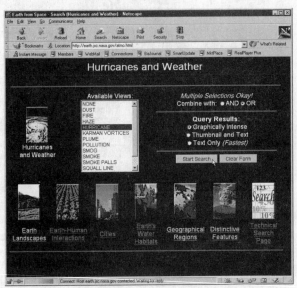

Saving Files from Web Pages *(cont.)*

In this instance, there is only one photograph in the database at this time. It is a photo of Hurricane Elena in the Gulf of Mexico. You will see an option to select a Hi-Resolution photo or a Lo-Resolution photo. Unless you have a very fast Internet connection, do **not** select Hi-Resolution. The photos are larger than what you would need for most projects and will take a long time to download.

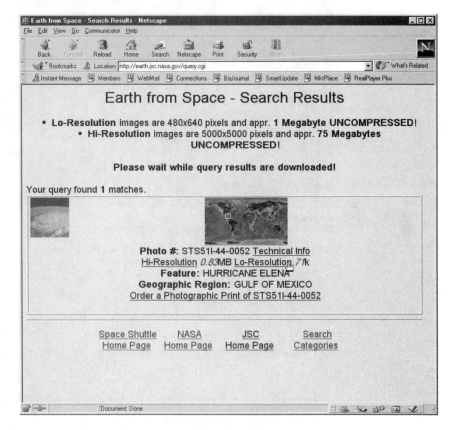

6. Click the ***Lo-Resolution*** hypertext link.

You will need to wait just a few minutes for the graphic to fully load into your browser.

Saving Files from Web Pages *(cont.)*

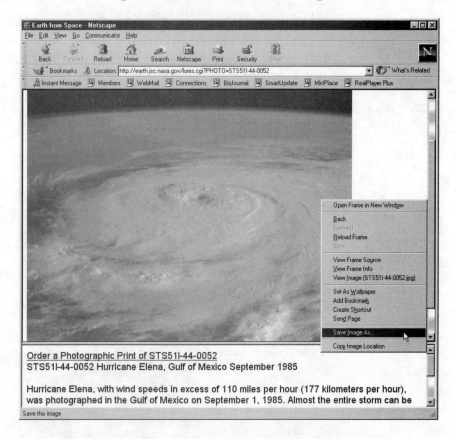

You will see that this database has information about each photograph in a separate frame in your *Navigator* window. You may want to print this information or have your students take notes from it while you are at the Web page.

In order to save the photograph to a folder on your hard drive or to a diskette, follow these steps.

7. Right-click the photograph.
8. On the menu that pops up, select ***Save Image As***.

Saving Files from Web Pages *(cont.)*

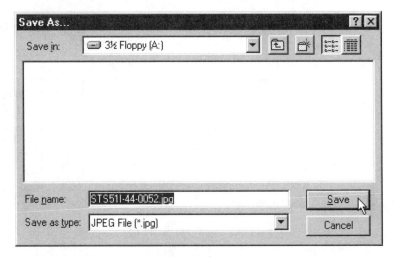

9. Select the folder or disk location where the image will be saved. The image will have a file name already assigned to it. This file has a numerical database file name. You can rename the file to make it easier to identify each image.

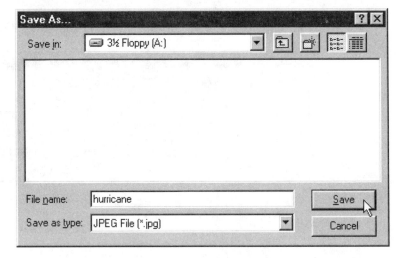

10. Renaming this file *hurricane* will help you remember that it is the hurricane photograph. You could also name it *Elena*.

11. Click the *Save* button when you are ready to save the photograph file.

Saving Files from Web Pages *(cont.)*

Once you have saved an image, you can transport it to another computer and use it in different programs that can use that image format.

Images used in Web pages are usually either GIF (Graphics Interchange Format) or JPG/JPEG (Joint Photographic Experts Group) format.

In order to view a GIF or JPG graphic, you can use *Netscape Navigator*.

12. Click *File*.
13. Click *Open Page*.

14. Click the *Choose File* button on the *Open Page* dialog box.

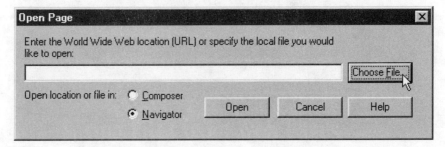

Saving Files from Web Pages *(cont.)*

15. In the ***Open*** dialog box, click to view the ***Files of type***: drop-down menu. Select ***All Files*** so that you can see graphics files as well as the HTML files.

16. Select the *hurricane.jpg* file that was saved.

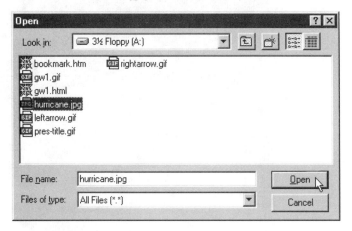

17. Click the ***Open*** button.

Saving Files from Web Pages *(cont.)*

18. Click the **Open** button on the **Open Page** dialog box.

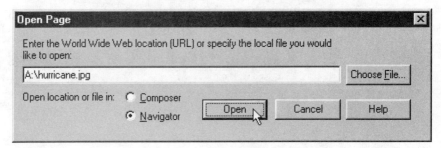

You should now see the hurricane photograph image in your *Navigator* window. If you have another graphics program, you can resize this image and change the file type for use in a multimedia program. Many of the new programs are accepting GIF or JPG graphics as file formats, so you may not have to change the file type.

Saving Files from Web Pages *(cont.)*

Graphic images are not the only files that can be saved to your hard drive or to a diskette. Sound files, program files, and multimedia program files can also be saved.

If you visit the **Kid's and Youth Educational Page** from the FBI, you will be able to listen to their weekly Radio Show.

1. Key this URL into the Location Box and press the *Enter* key:

   http://www.fbi.gov/kids/kids.htm

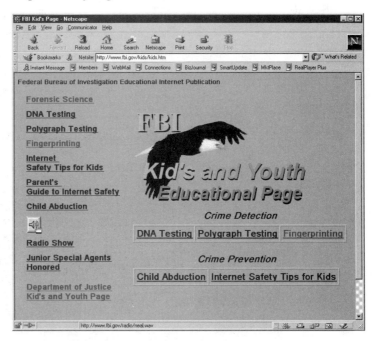

2. Click the sound icon button to hear a recorded message from the Radio Show.

You may see this small *Netscape* window open as the sound file is loaded. When the file has completely loaded into your memory, you will hear the weekly Radio Show.

Saving Files from Web Pages *(cont.)*

3. You can also click the hypertext link just below the button to read the transcript of the sound file.

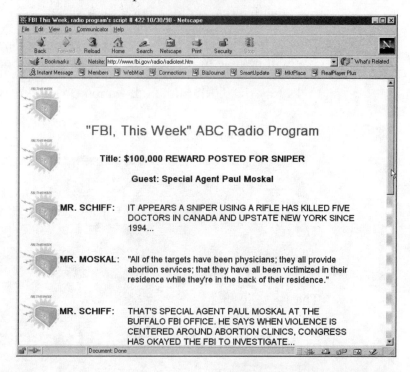

4. To save this (or any other sound file) right-click the button or hyperlink.

You will see this pop-up menu appear.

5. Click *Save Link As*.

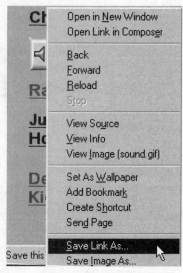

Saving Files from Web Pages *(cont.)*

6. Select the folder or diskette where the file will be saved.

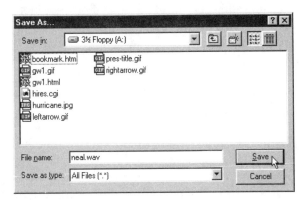

7. Click the *Save* button on the *Save As* dialog box.

The file is now saved and can be played on any computer with a sound player. This type of program usually comes with your sound card. You could also open the file in *Netscape Navigator*.

The **FBI kids** Web site also has instructional material about DNA testing, fingerprinting, polygraph testing, and other topics.

The fingerprinting Web page has super images of the basic types of fingerprints.

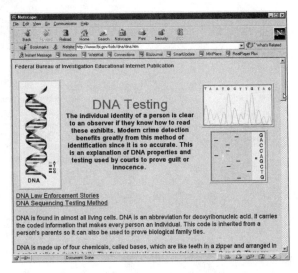

Saving Files from Web Pages *(cont.)*

You can also save movie files from Web sites to use on your computer at school as part of your lessons. *QuickTime* movies (.mov files) can be used in *HyperStudio* cards as part of a student's multimedia presentation.

Saving movie files to your hard drive greatly reduces the time you and your students will have to wait for the file to download from the Internet.

For example, the **Federal Emergency Management Agency** has a Web site for students.

1. Key this URL into the Location Box and press the ***Enter*** key:

   http://www.fema.gov/kids/

You should see the **FEMA for kids** Web page.

Saving Files from Web Pages *(cont.)*

There are many games and puzzles for students to use to learn how to prepare for emergencies.

2. Click the *FEMA Headline News* graphic hyperlink to go to a list of activities and graphics.

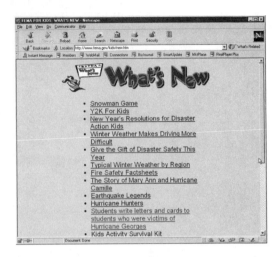

3. Scroll down the page until you see the hyperlink for *Hurricane and Tornado Videos*.

There are *RealMedia* and *QuickTime* movie files available for you to view. *RealMedia* files will be discussed in the Helper Applications section of this book.

4. Scroll down the page until you find the hyperlink for the *Tornado QuickTime* video.

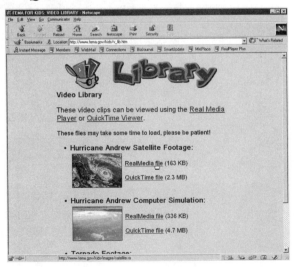

Saving Files from Web Pages *(cont.)*

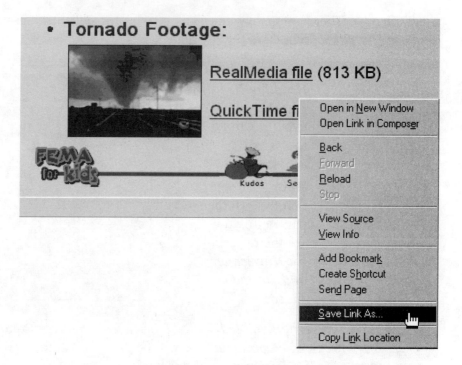

5. Right-click the hyperlink for the *QuickTime* file.
6. Select ***Save Link As*** from the pop-up menu.

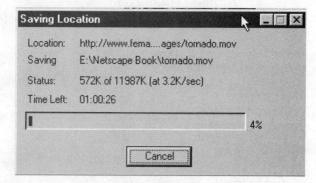

The download time from the Internet for a 33.6 modem is about an hour. This would not be a very useful lesson for your students if you had to wait an hour for the file to appear on your computer.

Saving Files from Web Pages *(cont.)*

Once you have saved the movie file to your hard drive, you can then open it in Navigator.

7. Click ***Open Page*** from the ***File*** menu.

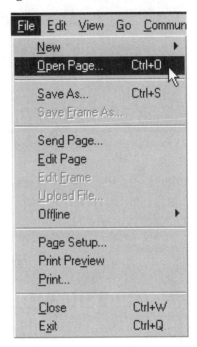

8. Find the correct file from the ***Open Page*** dialog box.

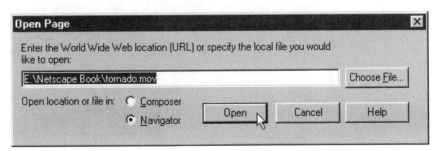

The movie will now load quickly from your hard drive. You and your students will be able to view it without waiting for an hour.

Saving Files from Web Pages *(cont.)*

You will notice that the file name in the Location Box shows that the file is located on your hard drive in the folder where you saved it.

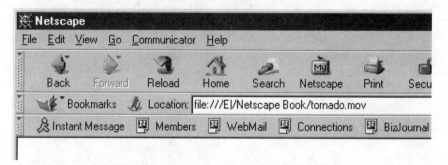

9. Click the **Play** button on the *QuickTime* controls to start playing the video clip.

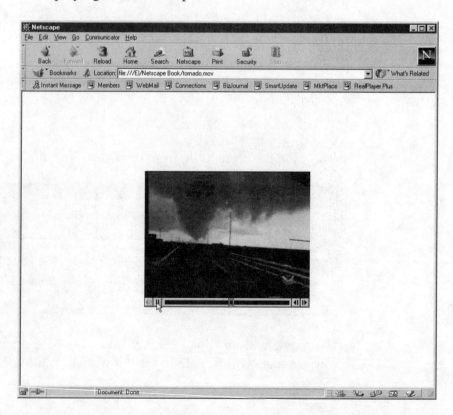

Using Plug-Ins

Plug-Ins are programs that you download from the World Wide Web. They work within *Netscape Navigator* to help you view special files such as movie files and virtual reality files.

One such plug-in is the *QuickTime* movie viewer from Apple Computer, Inc. This plug-in is used to view .mov movie files.

1. Key this URL into the Location Box and press the *Enter* key.

   http://starchild.gsfc.nasa.gov/docs/StarChild/StarChild.html

It will take you to the welcome Web page for the **StarChild** site.

2. Click the *Level 2 Solar System* hyperlink.

Using Plug-Ins *(cont.)*

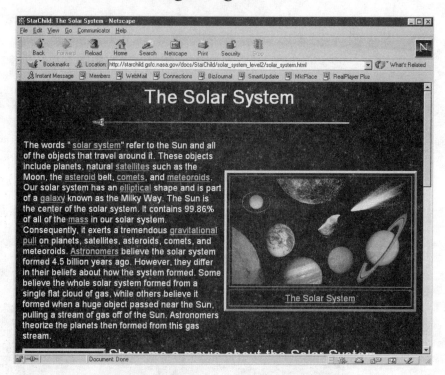

There are many hypertext links on these Web pages that will take you to additional information about the solar system.

3. Scroll down the page until you find the links for the movies.

There are two movies available, an AVI format movie and a *QuickTime* (MOV) format movie. In order for you to play the *QuickTime* movie, you must have the *QuickTime* plug-in installed.

You can find it at the **Apple Computer, Inc**. Web site:

http://www.apple.com/quicktime/

Follow the directions for downloading and installing the plug-in program.

Using Plug-Ins *(cont.)*

Once you have the plug-in installed, you can view the *QuickTime* movie.

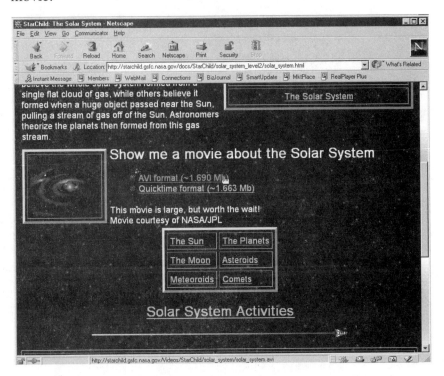

4. Click the hypertext link for the *QuickTime* format movie.

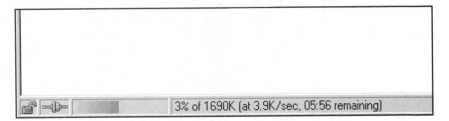

As it downloads, you will be able to watch the status of the download and how much time is remaining to complete the download. This will appear at the bottom of your Navigator window in the Status Bar.

Using Plug-Ins *(cont.)*

Until the file is completely downloaded, you will see this icon in the center of your *Navigator* window.

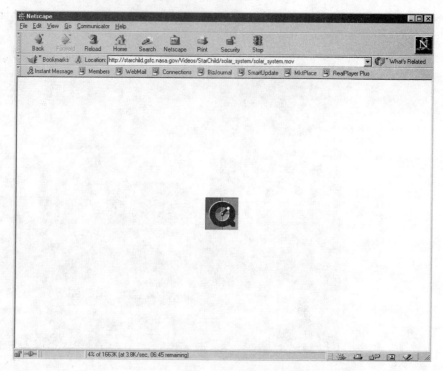

If you do not have the *QuickTime* plug-in installed correctly, you may see this graphic image in your *Navigator* window. This means that the file cannot play or that the file did not download correctly.

Using Plug-Ins *(cont.)*

When the download is complete, you will see the movie appear in the center of your *Navigator* window. You can use the *QuickTime* controls just beneath the movie to control sound, playing/pausing, and fast forward or rewind.

If you clicked on the AVI format movie, it would appear in the upper left-hand corner of your *Navigator* window. To play it, click the window. To pause it, click the window again.

Using Plug-Ins *(cont.)*

Another plug-in program is the ***Cosmo VRML*** player by CosmoSoftware. It is designed to play VRML (Virtual Reality Modeling Language) files. The program can be downloaded from the **CosmoSoftware** Web site.

> *http://cosmosoftware.com/*

Once you have installed the player, you can visit many Web sites with virtual reality interactive graphics. Here are some examples of what you and your students will find.

The **Virtual Polyhedra** site has a variety of geometric shapes that your students can view from all sides by manipulating the image in the viewer.

1. The site is at the URL:

> *http://www.li.net/%7Egeorge/virtual-polyhedra/vp.html*

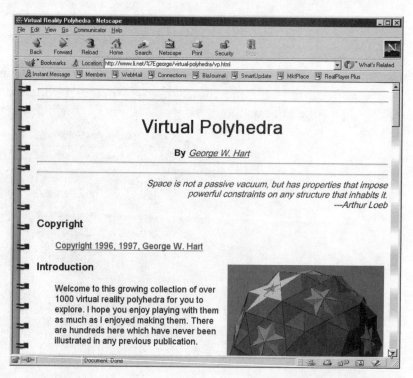

Using Plug-Ins *(cont.)*

There are geometric shapes in a variety of categories.

2. Click one of the lists of models.

3. Click an image name to open that file.

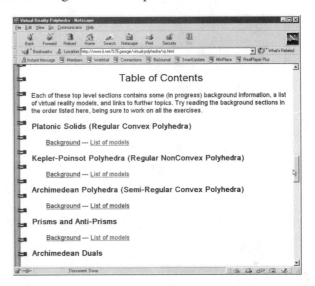

4. Once the image is loaded, you can rotate, zoom in, spin, and tilt it, using the *Cosmo* plug-in program.

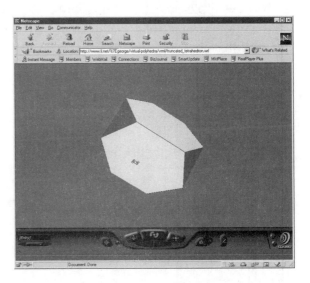

Using Plug-Ins *(cont.)*

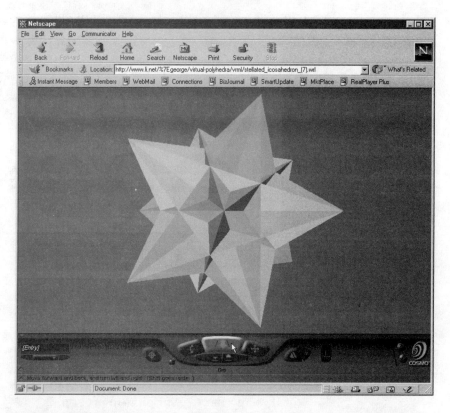

From simple objects to this more elaborate shape, the images are a terrific resource for any math class. There is also background information about the images and instructions for making some paper models.

Another Web site with geometric shapes for students to manipulate is the **MathMol K–12 Activity Page**. There are hypermedia textbooks and a quick tour of the Web site. Your students will enjoy the 3-D model images.

1. Enter this URL to go to the Web site.

   http://www.nyu.edu/pages/mathmol/K_12.html

Using Plug-Ins *(cont.)*

The **MathMol** site has molecular and geometric models for you and your students to manipulate.

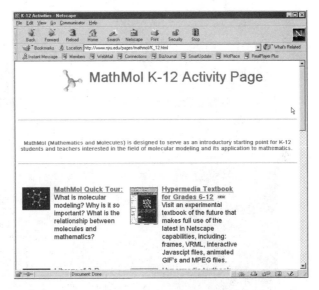

2. Scroll down the Web page until you find the hypertext links for the libraries of Geometric and Molecular Structures.

3. Click the *Geometric Structures* hyperlink.

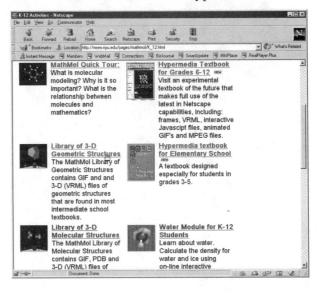

Using Plug-Ins *(cont.)*

There are plane surfaces such as circle, triangle, or rectangle. These are good examples to show two-dimensional surfaces.

4. Click the ***3-D Figures Library*** hyperlink on this page.

There are 3-D shapes such as a cone, dodecahedron, cube, cylinder, and sphere.

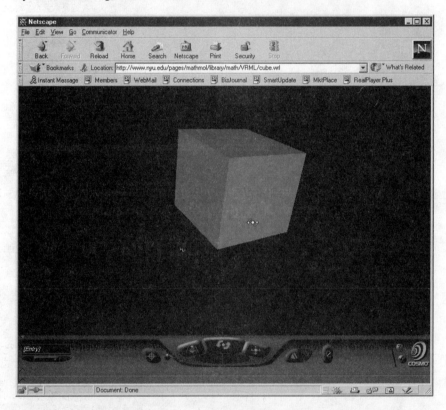

Once you make a choice, the object will appear in your *Netscape* window if the *Cosmo* plug-in software is working. This is an excellent way to demonstrate many different shapes to your students.

Using Plug-Ins *(cont.)*

The *Library of 3-D Molecular Structures* has a database for Water and Ice, Carbons, Hydrocarbons, Molecules of Life, and Drugs.

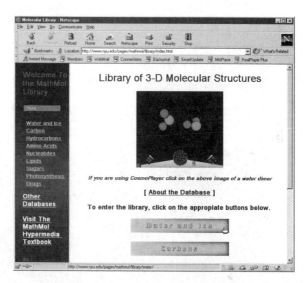

Select *Water and Ice* to view those molecules. This part of the Web site offers your students a chance to manipulate molecular models.

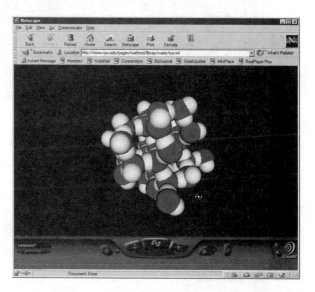

Using Plug-Ins *(cont.)*

Another Web site with 3-D VRML files is the **Earth in VRML**
Web site.

1. Key the URL into the Location Box and press the ***Enter*** key.

    http://vrml.gsfc.nasa.gov/

This Web site contains various images of Earth that will allow
your students to take a different look at our planet.

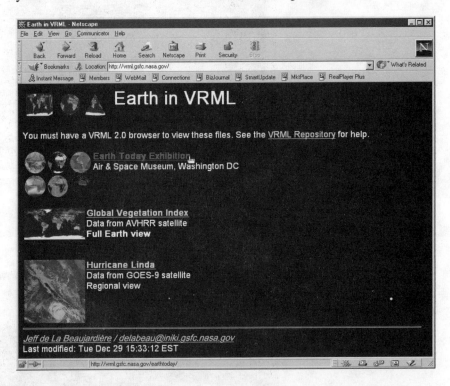

2. Click the hyperlink for the ***Earth Today Exhibition***. This
   will take you to a Web page with viewing choices for the
   earth models.

3. If you want all six globes to appear in your *Navigator*
   window, select the three-across, two-down view option.

Using Plug-Ins *(cont.)*

You will see six views of Earth. There is a normal view from space taken from the Galileo Spacecraft, Ocean Temperatures, Earth's Crust, and several others.

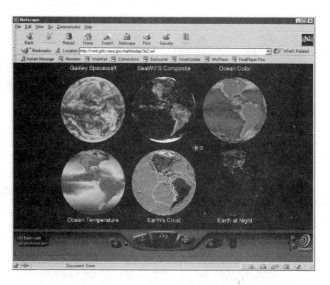

You can zoom in on any of the models. You can even spin and rotate them so that your view is from the top, bottom, or any angle from Earth's normal rotation.

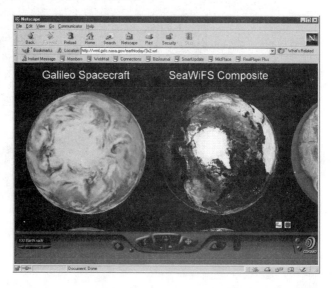

Using Plug-Ins *(cont.)*

The ***Global Vegetation Index*** shows an image of the Earth with vegetation areas in different colors. Your students can view any of the continents from a variety of angles.

The hyperlink for the *Hurricane Linda* images will link you to a Web page with several types of images of this hurricane.

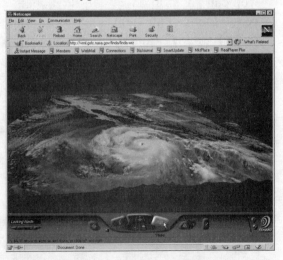

4. Select the VRML image so that your students can manipulate the 3-D model of a hurricane.

Using Plug-Ins *(cont.)*

If you are teaching a unit about the solar system, you might want to take your students to this Web site.

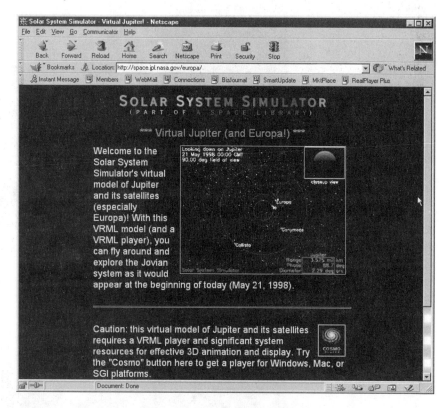

This Web page is part of the **Solar System Simulator** project. It is called Virtual Jupiter (and Europa!). You can find it at the URL:

http://space.jpl.nasa.gov/europa/
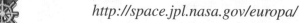

Your students will be able to manipulate Jupiter and its moons in the VRML viewer. This will give them an opportunity to view the orbits of the moons from different angles.

1. Once you go to the Web site, click the hyperlink *Show me Virtual Jupiter!*

Using Plug-Ins *(cont.)*

2. Each satellite (or moon) is labeled and is shown on its orbital path. Your students can zoom in on the planet.

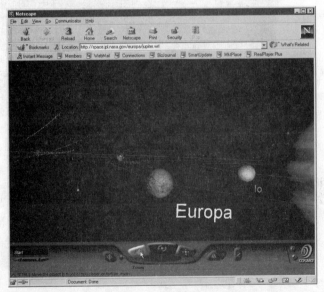

3. They can even zoom in on the satellites to see the various surfaces.

Using Plug-Ins *(cont.)*

The Jupiter model is the only VRML file at this site, but there are many other images your students can view or create at the **Solar System Simulator** main Web page.

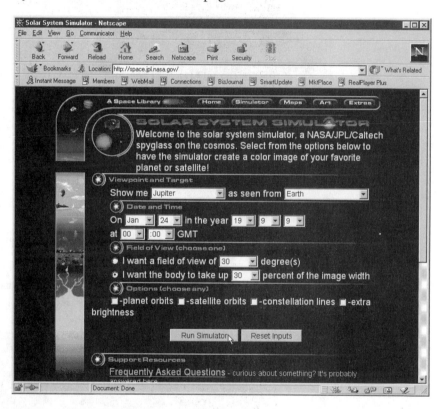

1. Click the hyperlink from the Jupiter page or key in this URL to go to the **Solar System Simulator**.

   http://space.jpl.nasa.gov/

2. Select the object you wish to view and the location from which you want to view it.

3. Next select the date and the time of the observation. You can also include planet and satellite orbits if you wish.

Using Plug-Ins *(cont.)*

4. Click the ***Run Simulation*** button.

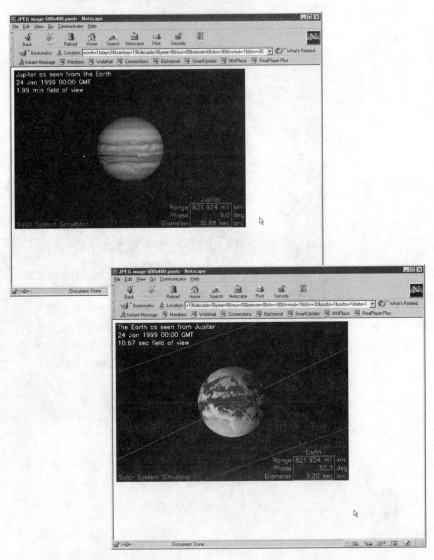

The simulation program will generate a photographic image with your specifications.

5. You can then save that image to your hard drive or a diskette, following the directions for saving a graphic.

Using Plug-Ins *(cont.)*

Another Web site to visit, if you are teaching about the planets, is the **Mars Pathfinder** Web site. It also has virtual reality models so you and your students can view where the Pathfinder landed and where the Rover traveled on the surface of Mars.

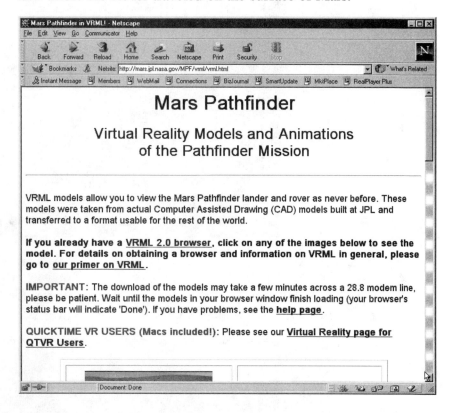

1. The **Mars Pathfinder in VRML** Web site is located at the URL:

   http://mars.jpl.nasa.gov/MPF/vrml/vrml.html

2. Scroll down the Web page to see the various image choices.

Using Plug-Ins *(cont.)*

3. The ***Virtual Reality in Panorama*** will give you a 360-degree panoramic view around the Mars Lander.

4. You can select the Lander and Rover on Mars to view animation of the landing and the opening of the Lander. It will also simulate movement of the Rover.

Using Plug-Ins *(cont.)*

There are several different views of the *Virtual Reality Terrain Models*. These allow you and your students various views of the landing site and the locations of the Rover as it traveled over the landing site's surface.

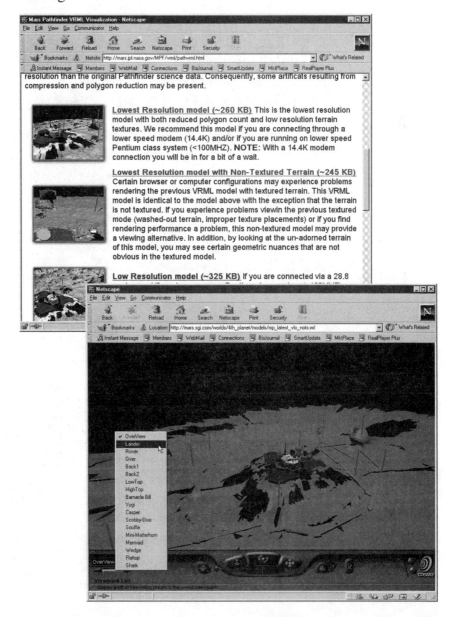

Using Plug-Ins *(cont.)*

The following sites are additional plug-in programs, and the locations where you can download them.

Chemscape Chime—MDL Information Systems
http://www.mdli.com/download/index.html

Chime enables viewing of "live" chemical structures.

Crescendo—LiveUpdate
http://www.liveupdate.com

This plug-in allows you to hear MIDI sound files.

HyperStudio Plug-In—Roger Wagner Publishing
http://www.hyperstudio.com/resource/hsplugin/plugin.html

This will allow you to view *HyperStudio* files which have been published on a Web page.

Shockwave—Macromedia
http://www.macromedia.com/shockwave/

This plug-in lets you view multimedia presentations and interactive Web content.

Flash3—Macromedia
http://www.macromedia.com/software/flash/

This is a viewer for animation and vector graphics.

Acrobat Reader—Adobe
http://www.adobe.com/

This plug-in will allow you to read and to print PDF (Portable Document Format) files.

Using Plug-Ins *(cont.)*

QuickTime VR—Apple Computers, Inc.
http://www.apple.com/quicktime/qtvr/index.html

This is a virtual reality viewer that allows you to view 3-D panoramic movies.

QuickView Plus—Word Viewer—Inso Corporation
http://www.inso.com/qvp/index.htm

This allows you to view Word documents in your *Netscape Navigator* window.

NetView—Dr. DWG
http://www.drdwg.com/webviewers/netview/index.html

This plug-in allows you to access and view AutoCAD(r) files in your browser.

VivoActive Player
http://www.vivo.com/products/playfree/vaplayer.html

This allows you to play streaming Vivo movie files.

BrowserWatch
http://browserwatch.internet.com/plug-in.html

This Web site maintains a large list of browser plug-in utilities. You may want to check here if you are trying to find a particular type of plug-in.

Web Browser Plug-Ins—My Shareware list
http://www.mysharewarepage.com/plugins.htm

This is another list of plug-in applications that you may want to check.

Helper Applications

A helper application is much like a plug-in program. It is used along with *Netscape Navigator* to allow you to view or listen to files you may find on the World Wide Web. Just as there are many plug-in programs, there are many helper application programs available. This section will highlight just a few.

The **Teacher Created Materials** Web site utilizes a helper application.

1. Key this URL into the Location Box and press the ***Enter*** key.

   http://www.teachercreated.com

This will take you to the **Teacher Created Materials** home page.

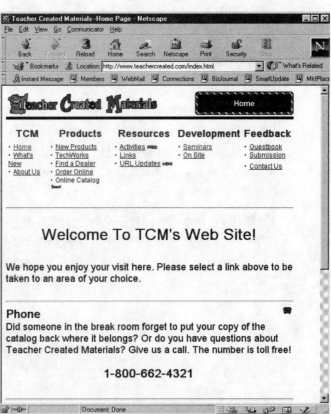

Helper Applications *(cont.)*

At the top of the screen, you will see a menu of available information.

2. Click the ***Activities*** hyperlink.

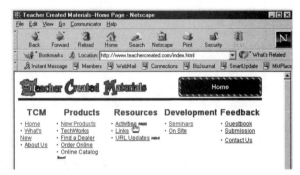

You will see the **Free Activities** Web page. Teacher Created Materials offers sample pages from some of their books each month. Visit this page often and download usable work sheets for your classes.

Helper Applications *(cont.)*

You must have the Adobe *Acrobat Reader* software to read the PDF (Portable Document Format) files.

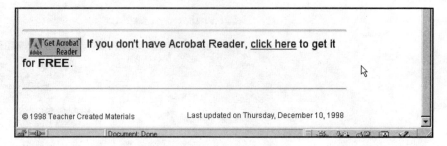

3. If you do not have this software installed on your computer, you can click the hyperlink and download it. It is available at this URL:

http://www.adobe.com/supportservice/custsupport/download.html

4. Once you have downloaded and installed the Reader application, you can click the hyperlink for an activity.

5. When asked whether you want to *Open* or *Save* the file, select *Open* and click the *OK* button.

To save the file to your hard drive, select the *Save it to disk* button.

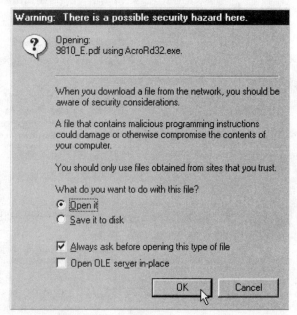

Helper Applications *(cont.)*

The Adobe *Acrobat Reader* program will open, and it will load the document from Teacher Created Materials.

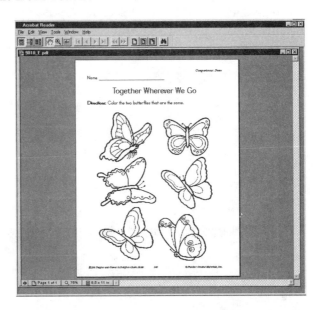

6. To print the work sheet, click the ***Print*** option in the ***File*** menu of the reader program.

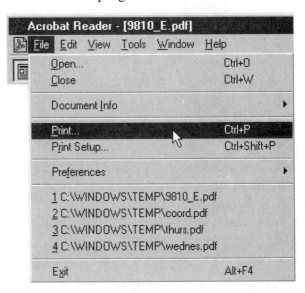

Helper Applications *(cont.)*

At the bottom of the *Acrobat Reader* window, you can see how many pages are in the document. This document has three pages. You can also see that this view of your document is set at 75% of the regular page size. You can click the size button and increase or decrease as needed.

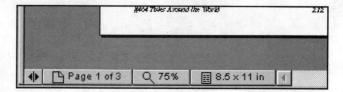

7. To move among the pages, click the arrows at the top of the window.

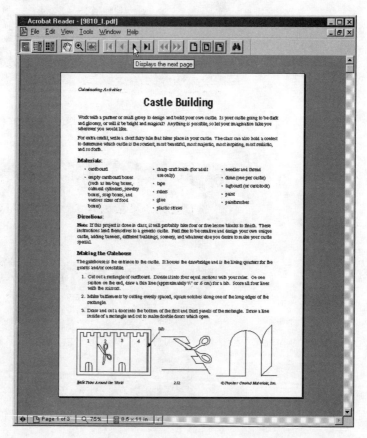

Helper Applications *(cont.)*

Another Web site that uses the PDF format to offer you a document is the **Kennedy Space Center Shuttle Launch** Web page.

It is located at this URL:

http://www-pao.ksc.nasa.gov/kscpao/schedule/schedule.htm

1. Click the hyperlink for the *Launch schedule in table format*.

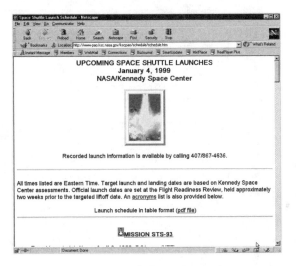

2. Select *Open it* to open the file, and click the *OK* button.

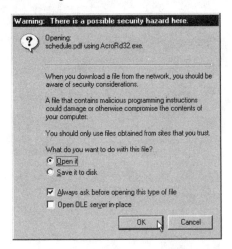

Helper Applications *(cont.)*

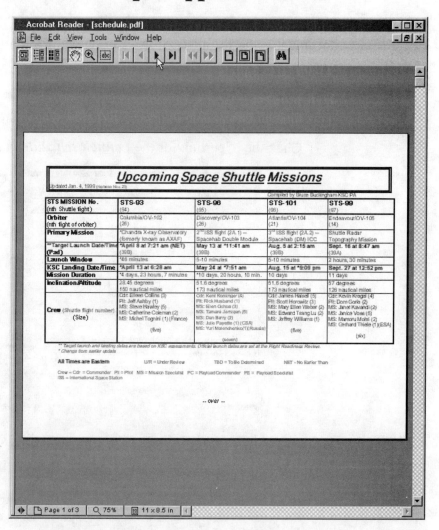

3. From this site you can print the schedule of shuttle missions for your classroom. It includes the orbiter name, the flight number of that orbiter, the scheduled launch and landing dates, the primary mission, and a list of the crewmembers.

Helper Applications *(cont.)*

The **Environmental Protection Agency's** Web site has many resources for teachers and students. The **EPA Explorers' Club** is located at the URL:

http://www.epa.gov/kids/

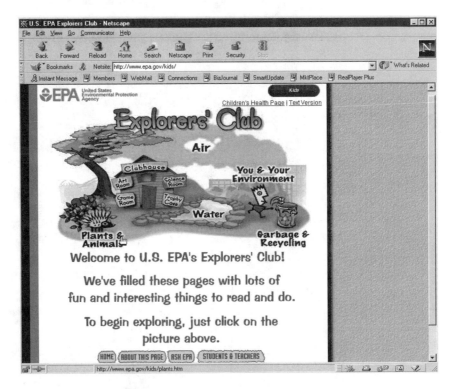

1. Click the graphic hyperlink for **Plants & Animals**.

This will take you to a Web page for younger students, with some activities about plants and animals in the environment.

Helper Applications *(cont.)*

2. Click the hyperlink to *Charlie Chipmunk*.

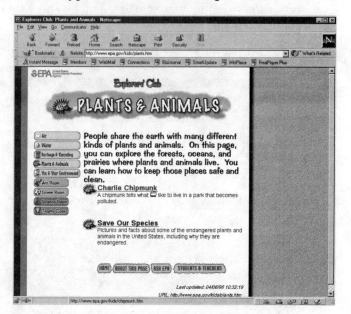

3. Click the hyperlink sentence about downloading a copy of the coloring book in PDF format.

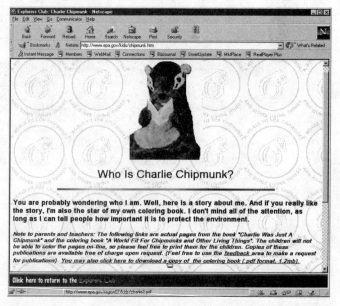

Helper Applications *(cont.)*

4. You can open the file or select **Save it to disk** in case you would like to print it on the printer at school.

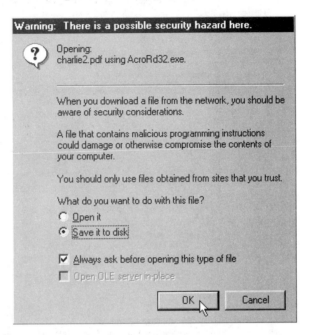

5. Select the folder where you want to save the file.

6. Click the **Save** button on the **Save As** dialog box.

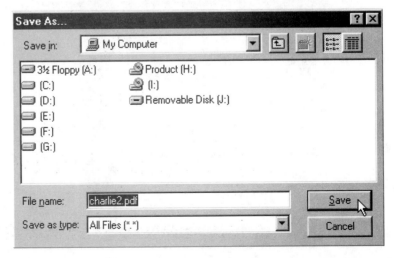

Helper Applications *(cont.)*

This is a 27-page coloring book about the animals that live in the woods. Once you have saved it, you can print pictures for your students while teaching about the conservation of our parks and woodlands.

Helper Applications *(cont.)*

The Environmental Protection Agency also has Web pages and activities for older students. These are located at their **EPA Student Center** Web site.

The site is located at the URL:

http://www.epa.gov/students/

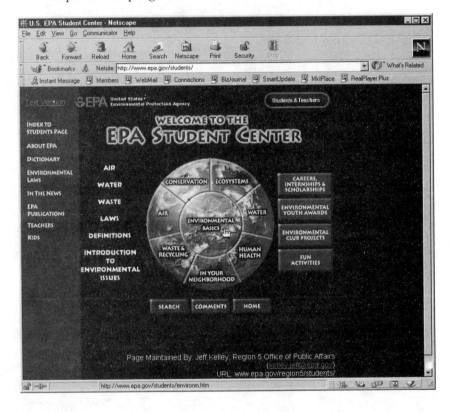

1. Click the different sections of the globe graphic to take you to that part of the Web site.
2. For this example, click the center section, ***Environmental Basics***.

Helper Applications *(cont.)*

3. Click the hyperlink to the **Guide to Environmental Issues**.

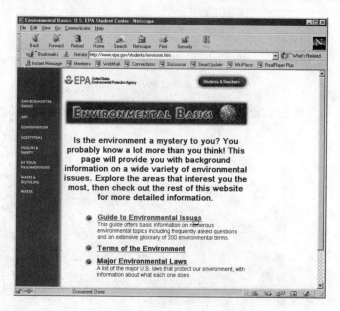

You will be able to download the PDF file for the EPA's guidebook to the most current environmental issues.

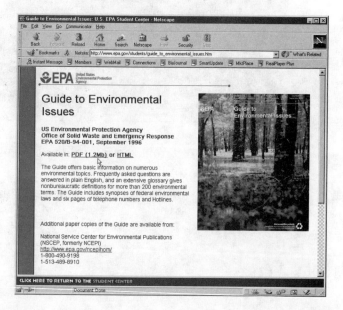

Helper Applications *(cont.)*

4. Once the guide is downloaded, it can be printed or read from the computer screen.

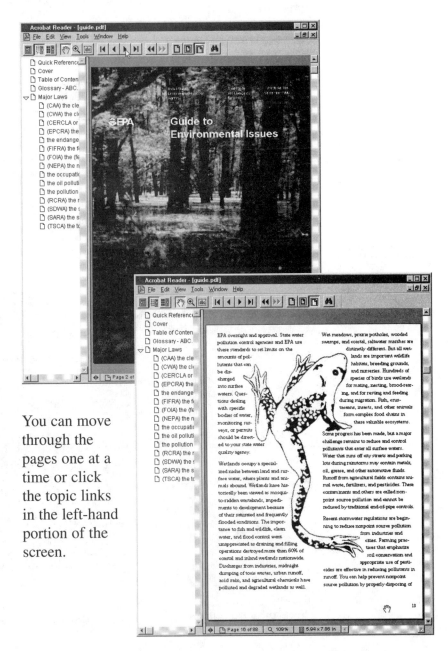

You can move through the pages one at a time or click the topic links in the left-hand portion of the screen.

Helper Applications *(cont.)*

Another helper application that installs when you install *Netscape Communicator* is the *AOL Instant Messenger*. This is a simple, messaging software that allows you to chat with other *AOL Instant Messenger* users and AOL subscribers.

1. Click the **Instant Message** button on your Button Bar.

2. Select **Open it** from the dialog box.

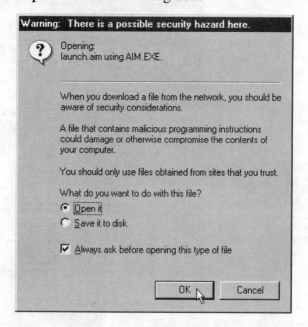

3. Click the **OK** button to start the program.

Helper Applications *(cont.)*

4. Click the *List Setup* tab.

5. Click the *Netscape AOL Instant Messenger* button to access the setup options.

6. Click *Options* on the pop-up menu.

7. Click *Edit Preferences*.

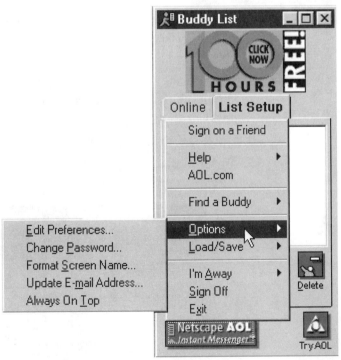

Helper Applications *(cont.)*

8. If you do **not** want *AIM* (*AOL Instant Messenger*) to start whenever Windows starts, click in the box to remove that check mark.

9. If you want to keep others from starting your *AIM*, you should click to remove the check mark beside *Save password*, also.

10. Click *OK* to set those options.

11. To set or change your screen name, select *Format Screen Name* from the *Options* menu.

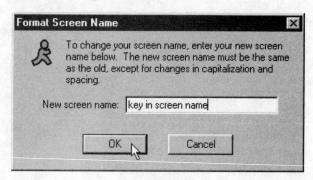

Helper Applications *(cont.)*

12. To add Buddies or other users to your list, click the **Add Buddy** button.

13. Key in the screen name or AOL user name and press the **Enter** key.

AIM will now let you know when your Buddies are online.

14. Click the **Buddies** heading to see a list of the users who are online.

15. Select the screen name and then the **IM** button to send a message to a particular user.

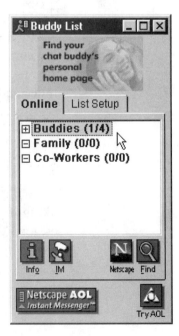

Helper Applications *(cont.)*

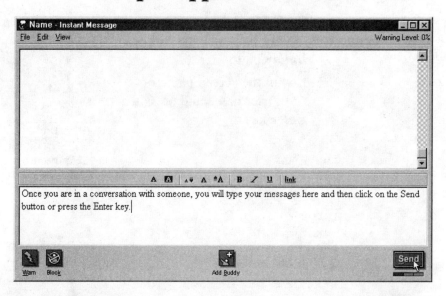

16. This is the message screen. You can key in your messages in the bottom part of the window.

17. Then click **Send** or press the **Enter** key to send the message to the other person.

18. To exit a chat session, simply click the *X* button in the top right-hand corner of the message window.

19. To exit *AIM*, click the *X* button in the top right-hand corner of the Buddy List box.

20. You will then see a dialog box asking if you want to close your session. Click the *Yes* button if you are ready to exit *AIM*.

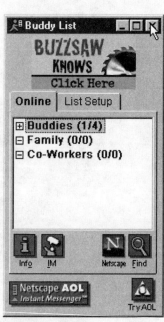

Helper Applications *(cont.)*

Another common helper application is the *RealPlayer* audio and video player from **RealNetworks**.

If you do not have this player, you can download the most recent version from their Web site at this URL:

http://www.real.com/

Once you have downloaded and installed the viewer software, you can view streaming movies and hear long audio files without waiting for them to load into your computer's memory. You do not need to save *RealVideo* movies to your hard drive. They play as you access them online.

The **Learning Technologies Channel Archive** from NASA has several movies archived. You can see the following Web pages about the Wright Flyer project at this URL:

http://quest.arc.nasa.gov/ltc/adto/wfo.html

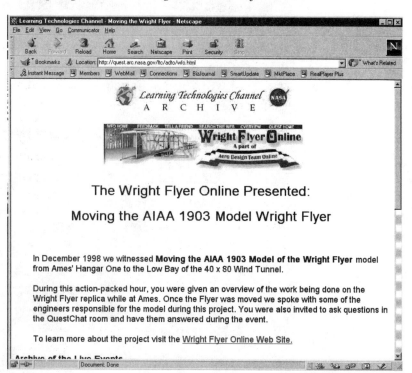

Helper Applications *(cont.)*

Scroll down the Web page and click the *RealVideo* version of the Archive of Events. You will see the video program about moving the model of the Wright flyer to the wind tunnel testing area.

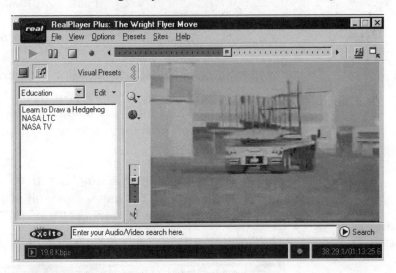

You and your students will view the moving of the full-scale model of the flyer as well as a discussion of what will be done with it. There will also be diagrams and small models to illustrate the discussion.

Helper Applications *(cont.)*

NASA TV is now being broadcast through the **Learning Technologies Channel** via the *RealPlayer*. Information can be found at this URL:

http://quest.arc.nasa.gov/ltc/live/

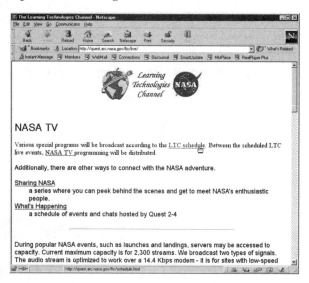

You and your students can view various broadcasts throughout the day. From shuttle launches to views of Earth from space, there is always something worthwhile being broadcast.

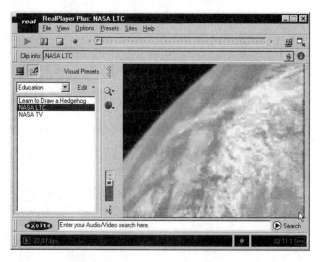

Helper Applications *(cont.)*

The **Learning Technologies Space Team Online** Web site has archived *RealVideos* of past launches and other space events. These are especially interesting if you and your students have not seen shuttle or rocket launches at night.

The **Space Team Online** Web page is at the URL:

http://quest.arc.nasa.gov/ltc/sto/launch/

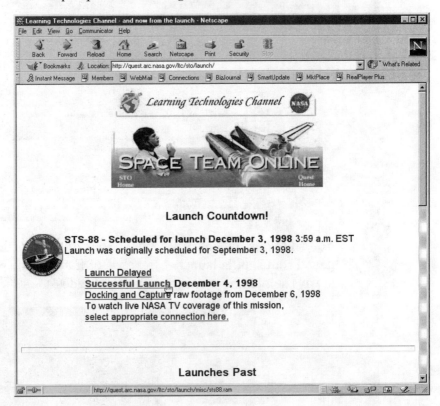

The STS-88 launch was at night, and the video will be sure to catch your students' attention.

Helper Applications *(cont.)*

From its pre-launch position on the launch pad through its ascent into space, the video of the STS-88 launch is breathtaking.

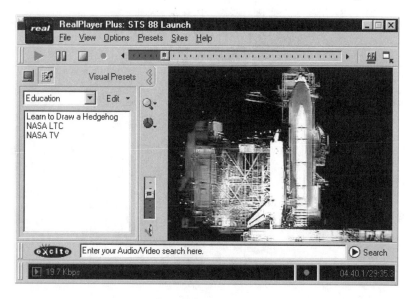

The video is a composite of various camera angles, so you are able to see everything that is happening.

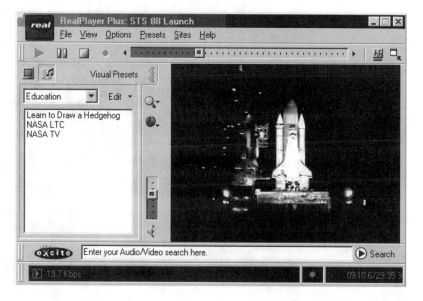

Helper Applications *(cont.)*

The close-up inset allows you to show your students what is happening during the launch process.

The video follows the shuttle through liftoff with information from ground control, as well.

Helper Applications *(cont.)*

The **NASA Connect** education project uses *RealVideo* movies and animations as a way for you and your students to view the programs.

NASA Connect is located at the URL:

http://edu.larc.nasa.gov/connect/

You may register and participate in the current program or view past activities.

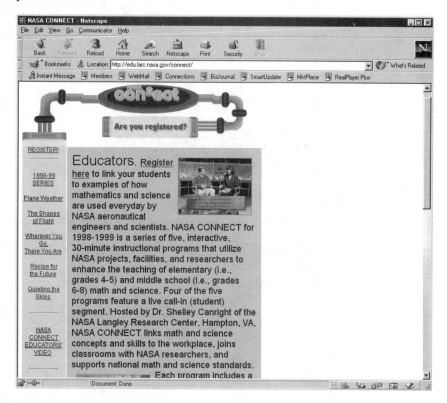

Helper Applications *(cont.)*

By clicking the video hyperlink, your *RealPlayer* will begin, and you and your students can view the movie or animation that accompanies the lesson.

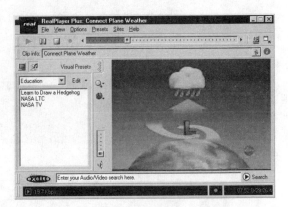

The print materials and lesson plans are available as a PDF file. You will need the Adobe *Acrobat Reader* to access that information.

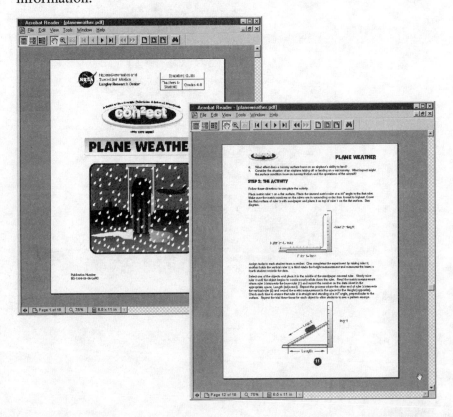

Helper Applications *(cont.)*

Another site, which has made good use of the *RealVideo* format, is **Jan Brett's Home Page**. Author of such books as *The Hat* and *The Mitten*, her Web site is a terrific place for teachers, parents, and students to visit.

It is located at this URL:

> *http://www.janbrett.com*

Along with lesson ideas, coloring pages, full-page mask graphics, and online postcards, Jan Brett has videotaped directions for drawing Hedgie the Hedgehog.

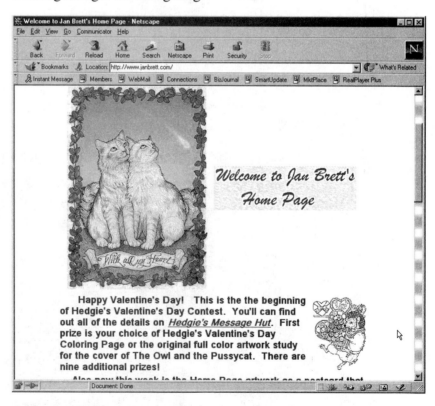

Scroll down her home page and click the button for the video, ***Learn to Draw a Hedgehog.***

Helper Applications *(cont.)*

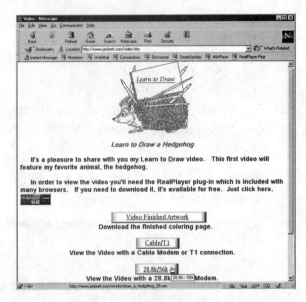

If you have a slower connection, you will need to click the button for *28.8k/56k*.

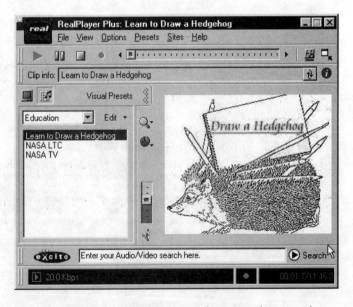

The video shows Jan Brett demonstrating step-by-step instructions for drawing Hedgie.

Helper Applications *(cont.)*

Here are some additional helper applications and the locations where you can find them.

ACDSee—ACD Systems
http://www.acdsystems.com

This helper allows viewing of various graphic file formats which your browser does not view. Will also allow file conversion and thumbnail viewing of graphic images in a folder.

LView Pro—MMedia Research Corp.
http://www.lview.com/

This program will help you view, edit, and create many types of graphic files, including BMP, PCX, TIFF, JPEG, and GIF files.

Windows Media Player—Microsoft
http://www.microsoft.com/windows/mediaplayer/download/default.asp

Player will open and play a large variety of audio and video file formats.

Winzip—Nico Mak Computing, Inc.
http://www.winzip.com/

This application allows you to compress or decompress zipped (PKZIP) files.

Streamworks Player—Xing Technology Corporation
http://www.xingtech.com/downloads/sw/

This helper application plays MPEG audio and video files.

NET TOOB—Digital Bitcasting Corporation
http://www.bitcasting.com/nettoob/

This program plays multimedia files such as MPEG-1, Video for Windows (AVI), QuickTime for Windows (MOV), QuickTime VR, Autodesk Animations (FLC/FLI), WAV audio, and MIDI audio.

Helper Applications *(cont.)*

MPEG for Real—Digital Bitcasting Corporation
http://www.duplexx.com/welcome.html

This helper application allows you to play MPEG movie files through your RealPlayer.

MidiGate—PRS Corporation
http://www.prs.net/prs/midigate.html

This is a helper application for playing MIDI audio files.

MiniCD, MiniWAV, MiniMedia, and MiniTEXT—The MiniAPPs
http://users.utu.fi/seaavi/minicd.html

These are applications that allow you to view or play a variety of multimedia file formats.

TUCOWS
http://www.tucows.com

This is a repository for shareware programs for Windows and Macintosh. You can search here for new helper applications.

Stroud's Consummate Winsock Applications
http://cws.internet.com/inx.html

This is another Windows application repository.

FilePile
http://filepile.com/nc/start

This is a collection of both Windows and Macintosh shareware files.

Shareware.Com
http://www.shareware.com/

This is another collection of multi-platform shareware where you can search for the latest helper applications.

Searching for Information

Now that you know how to use your browser, how do you find the information you need? There are Web sites with search capabilities to help you find that information.

One such site is **Excite**. It offers many services, but we will focus on the search engine. A search "engine" is a search mechanism that not only looks through a listing of Web sites but also searches for keywords and related words within those Web sites. It then returns to you a list of hyperlinks to Web pages that meet your criteria.

 It is located at the URL:

http://www.excite.com

The blank search box for the search engine is located at the top right of the Web page. You enter the keywords that you are researching and then click the **Search** button.

1. Key in *Aesop's fables*.
2. Click the **Search** button.

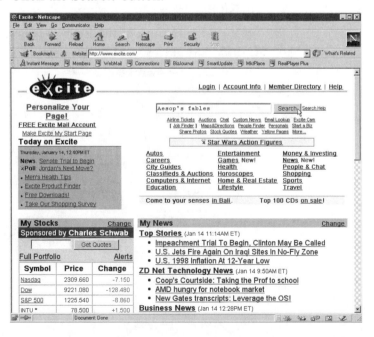

Searching for Information *(cont.)*

After several seconds, you will see a Web page that has the search's ***Web Results***. This is a list of Web sites that are about Aesop, fables, or related topics. The percentage listed is a guide as to how well this Web site matches your search criteria.

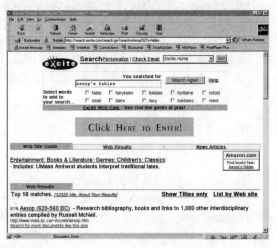

3. After reading the short summary, you can click the hyperlink to visit that Web site.

4. Scroll to the bottom of the Results page and click the ***Next Results*** button to see additional Web sites.

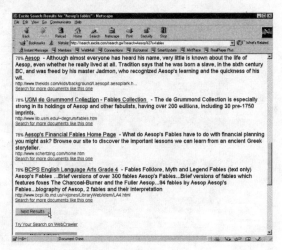

Searching for Information *(cont.)*

You can add to your search criteria by adding words to the search line. **Excite** offers suggested keywords that you can click to add to your search criteria.

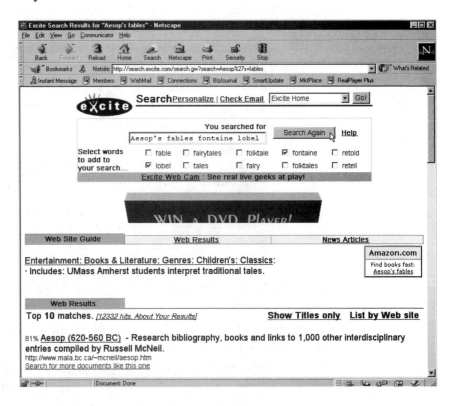

5. Click *fontaine* and *lobel* to add those authors to your search for fables or tales.

6. Click the *Search Again* button.

You should see a Web page with suggested Web sites for Aesop's fables and stories by Fontaine and Lobel.

Searching for Information *(cont.)*

For additional information about how you can refine your search strategy, check the Help page provided by most search engines. **Excite** has a hyperlink to Search Help.

7. Click *Search Help* to find this information.

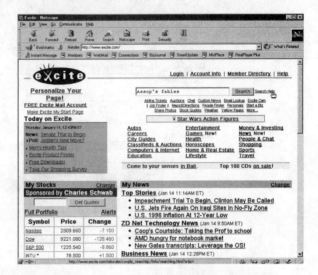

The Help page gives you additional information about what a search is and how to improve your search techniques.

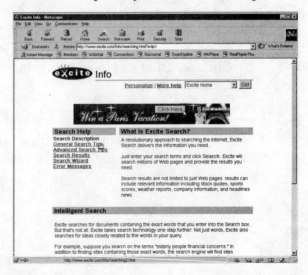

Searching for Information *(cont.)*

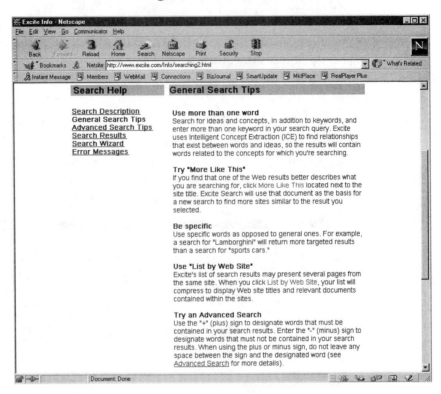

Some of their general search tips apply to other search engines as well. Try using some of these tactics:

- Use more than one word in the search window.
- Click the hyperlink for "More Like This" to see similar Web pages.
- Use specific words in your search.
- Use quotation marks around phrases to have the search engine look for the entire phrase.
- Use a + sign before words which **must** be in the search results and a - sign before words which you do **not** want to appear.

Searching for Information *(cont.)*

Another type of search Web site is a categorized list. One of the leading search lists is **Yahoo!**. When you use **Yahoo!**, you search through the categories of information.

It is located at the URL:

http://www.yahoo.com

On the main page, you will see a search form blank and a hyperlink for options. You will also see lists of major categories. You can either enter keywords for your search, or you can click one of the categories and follow the divisions.

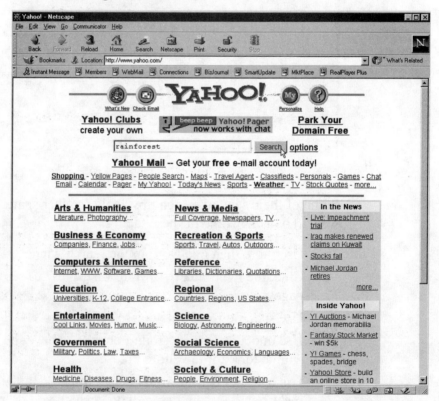

1. Key the word *rainforest* into the search blank.
2. Click the ***Search*** button.

Searching for Information *(cont.)*

The search results provide you with additional categories of information and a list of Web site matches.

3. Click the hyperlinks to travel to the Web sites.

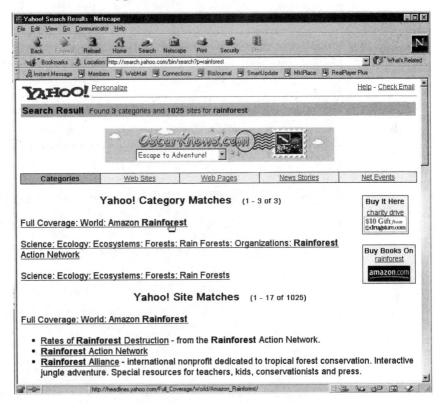

Keep in mind when you are searching that not all of the Web sites that appear in your search results will still be active Web sites. Some Web sites are no longer at the same address, or the server may change its address. It can take a while for that information to get to some of the search engines or lists.

Searching for Information *(cont.)*

4. To improve your search results on **Yahoo!**, click the ***options*** hyperlink.

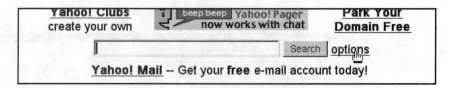

Here you can specify that you want to search for an exact phrase, find matches for all of your keywords, and find sites that were listed within a certain time frame. The time frame option will greatly increase the chances that the Web site will still be an active address.

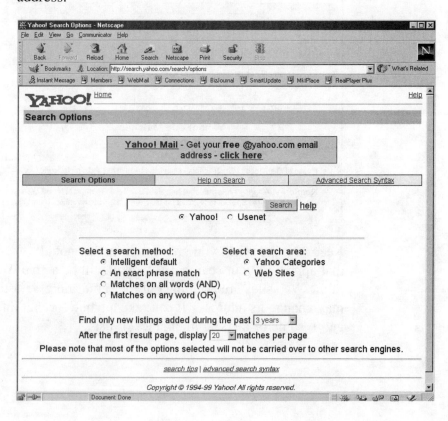

Searching for Information *(cont.)*

Yahoo! also offers its search capabilities to children. The **Yahooligans!** Web site is a safe place for you and your students to search for information.

It is located at the URL:

http://www.yahooligans.com

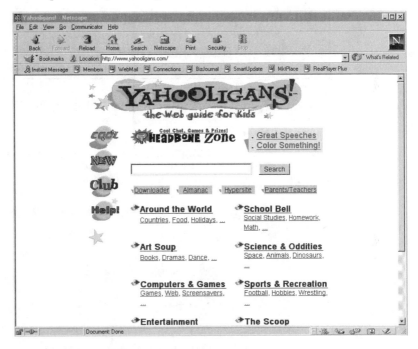

The ***Downloader*** hyperlink on the main page offers kids graphics, sounds, and video clips to download.

The ***Almanac*** link takes them to an almanac of facts for kids.

The ***Hypersite*** link takes kids to an interesting site of the week. There is an explanation of the site and a hyperlink for them to click.

The ***Parents/Teachers*** hyperlink will lead you to information about teaching with **Yahooligans!** and about teaching search strategies.

Searching for Information *(cont.)*

The main Web page includes a search blank as well as the category lists.

1. Enter the keyword *rainforest* into the search blank.

Click the **Search** button.

Notice the difference in the search results. These Web sites are geared toward students and schools.

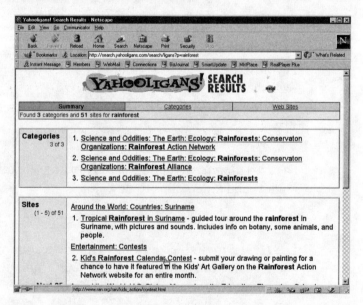

Each Web site listed also has a more lengthy explanation so that your students will be better able to select the Web site they need to visit.

Searching for Information *(cont.)*

If your students are interested in finding information about a listed category of Web sites, they can click the hyperlinks until they find the category they need.

2. Click the ***Around the World*** hyperlink.

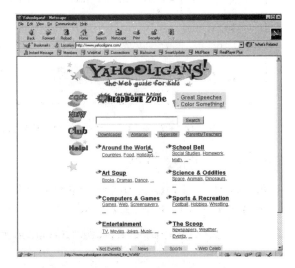

The next Web page is a list of categories and also tells how many Web sites in each category. ***Around the World*** leads you to categories such as Archeology, Cultures, Flags, Languages, and Travel.

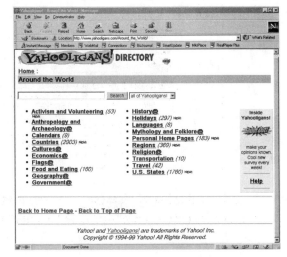

Searching for Information *(cont.)*

Another search Web site for students is the **Ask Jeeves for Kids!** site. This site lets kids ask questions about a variety of topics.

It is located at the URL:

 http://www.ajkids.com/

In order to search for information, enter a question into the search blank and click the *Ask* button.

The response Web page will provide other leading questions to narrow the search criteria. Students can select the link that best fits their question.

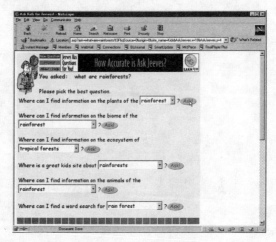

Searching for Information *(cont.)*

Clicking one of the questions will lead students to a Web page about that topic. These Web pages are from a variety of resources.

At the bottom of the response Web page, students will find the results from searches by several other search engines. These Web sites have been approved through the online filter *Surf-Watch*. Students can click a drop-down menu and choose from those recommended Web sites.

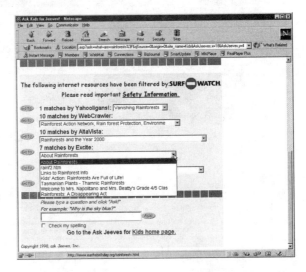

Searching for Information *(cont.)*

The leading questions are different, depending on the initial topic. The resource Web sites offer a quick way for students to find information about their questions.

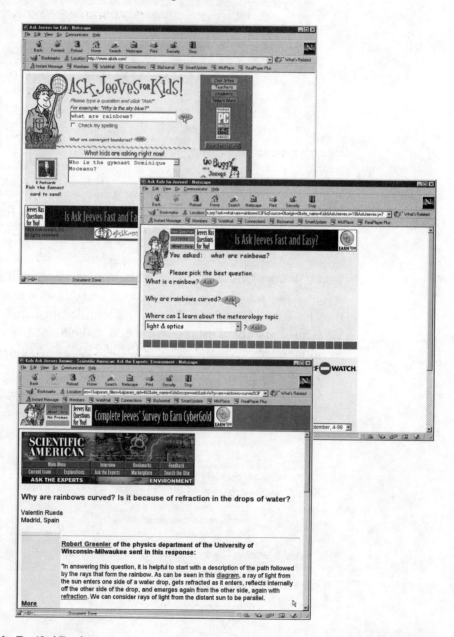

Searching for Information *(cont.)*

The **Ask Jeeves for Kids!** Web site also offers teacher and student resources. By clicking the buttons for **Teachers** or **Students**, you can access other sites that have been picked out by Jeeves.

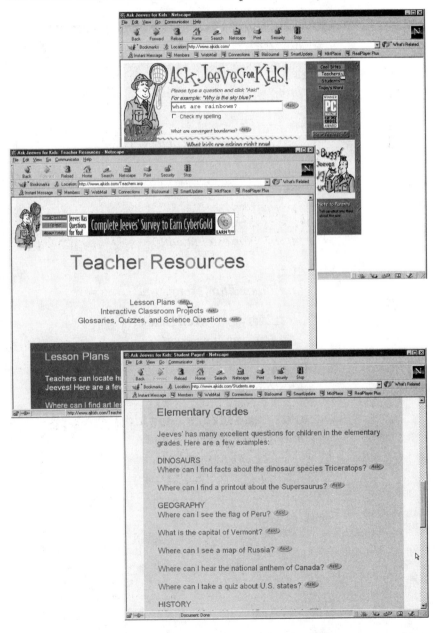

Searching for Information *(cont.)*

There are many search engines and lists online. Different lists sometimes have different Web pages listed. Here are the URLs of some you may want to try.

AltaVista
> *http://www.altavista.com/*

Google
> *http://www.google.com/*

HotBot
> *http://www.hotbot.com/*

Infoseek
> *http://infoseek.go.com/*

Lycos
> *http://lycos.cs.cmu.edu/*

Magellan
> *http://magellan.excite.com/*

Microsoft Network Web Search
> *http://search.msn.com/*

Pathfinder
> *http://www.pathfinder.com/search/altavista/*

PeachPod (search engine for kids)
> *http://www.peachpod.com/*

Starting Point
> *http://www.stpt.com/*

WebCrawler
> *http://www.webcrawler.com/*

Using Online Forms

As you visit various Web sites on the World Wide Web, you will encounter some that ask you to fill in blanks and submit information. A good rule is to be wary of what sites are asking for what information. You should also instruct your students to never fill out forms with their personal information such as name, address, or phone number.

There will be times, however, when you want to subscribe to a mailing list, order software or merchandise, or enter data into a project Web site.

The Landmark Project Web site has a wonderful project that was started back in 1987. It is called the Global Grocery List.

The Landmark Project site is at this URL:

http://www.landmark-project.com/home.html

Landmarks for Schools Web site is at:

http://www.landmark-project.com/

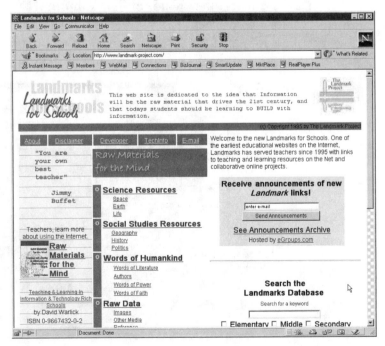

Using Online Forms *(cont.)*

To access the **Global Grocery List Project**, scroll to the bottom of the Web page and click the hyperlink.

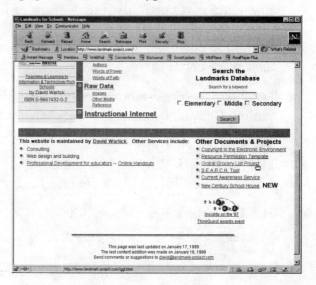

David Warlick, the creator of **The Landmark Project** Web site, created this project in 1987 in an effort to have students collaborate over the Internet and share real data that could be analyzed by students in a variety of curriculum areas.

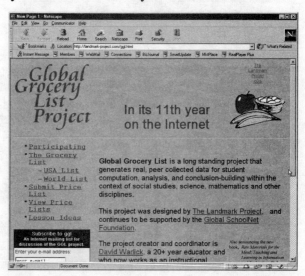

Using Online Forms *(cont.)*

Your students collect data about local grocery prices. They enter this information into the main database from the Web site. They can then retrieve data from many cities and countries to compare/contrast food prices. Your students should be able to draw some conclusions about agriculture and marketing based on some of the prices.

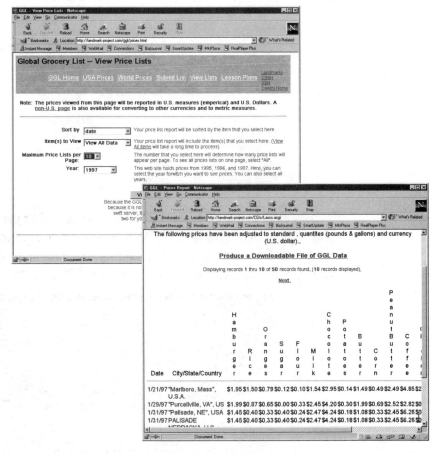

You can choose to view the prices of some or all of the data. The search can be limited to a specific year and a maximum number of records per reply. The reply to your query is organized according to location. The prices are set in columns so that you and your students can read them easily.

Using Online Forms *(cont.)*

To submit your information, have your students find the prices of the items on the grocery list for your location. You may want to average prices from different stores to get a class price. You then must enter the data into the database. This is done through a form located on the Web site.

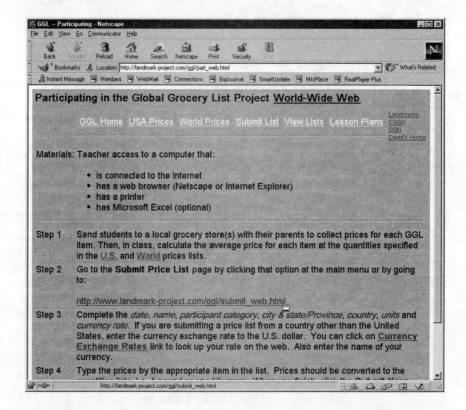

1. Click the hyperlink to go to the *Submit Price* Web page.

Using Online Forms *(cont.)*

2. Students should enter data about their location and when they collected their prices.

3. Use the *Tab* key to move from blank to blank within the form.

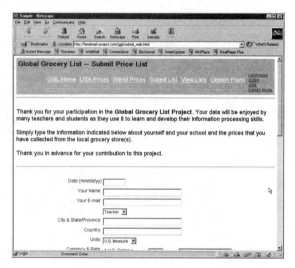

4. Scroll down the page and enter all of the prices.

5. When students are finished entering the prices, click the *Submit Your Price List* button.

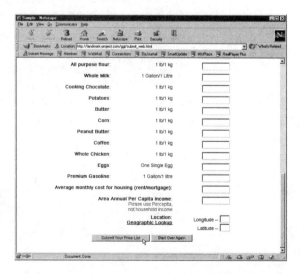

Using Online Forms *(cont.)*

In addition to the Global Grocery List, **The Landmark Project** Web site has many resources for teachers and students.

Select a heading on the **Landmarks for Schools** Web page, and you will find resources for integrating Web sites into your curriculum.

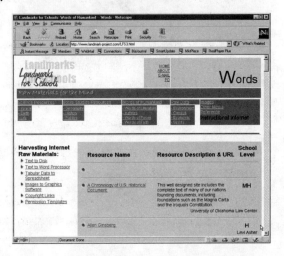

The **New Century School House** is a project that allows teachers to share their ideas and dreams about what schools in the future should be like. Visit some of the rooms in the schoolhouse or "occupy" a room that you have created with your own ideas.

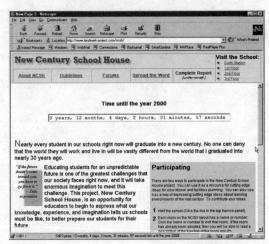

Webcams—Your Window to the World

There are many sites on the Web that have automatically reloading camera images of various objects or locations. These are called "Webcams." They are software-run cameras that take a picture at a designated interval of time. The software then uploads the image to a Web page.

You do not need any special software or plug-ins to view Webcam images. They will appear in the associated Web page window. Some of the Web pages will reload automatically so that you see the new image with each picture taken. On other pages, you will have to click your **Reload** button to view the newest image.

The following are some examples of Webcams you and your students can visit.

The **Washington State Department of Transportation** has a Web site that has image maps with markers that show various Webcams along the freeways of the Puget Sound area.

The Web site is located at this URL:

http://www.wsdot.wa.gov/regions/northwest/NWFLOW/camera/

Click the buttons to switch views from Seattle to Tacoma.

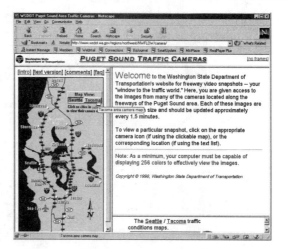

Webcams—Your Window
to the World *(cont.)*

Click the camera graphics on the image map to see the different camera views.

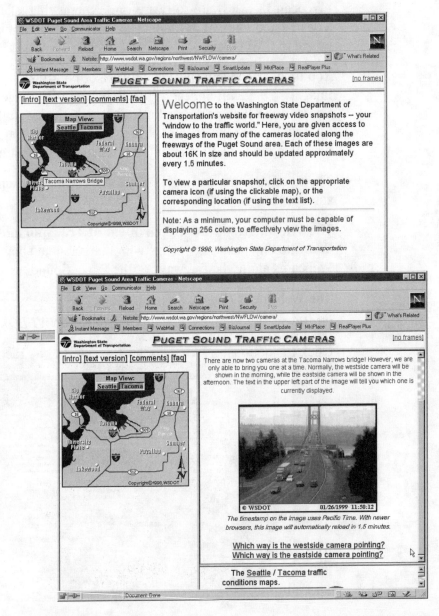

Webcams—Your Window
to the World *(cont.)*

The **National Weather Service** in Grand Junction, Colorado, maintains a Webcam with an image from the top of Grand Mesa.

http://www.crh.noaa.gov/gjt/index.html

Scroll down the page and click the ***Weather Camera*** hyperlink.

Webcams such as this one are great tools for showing weather differences in various parts of the country and around the world.

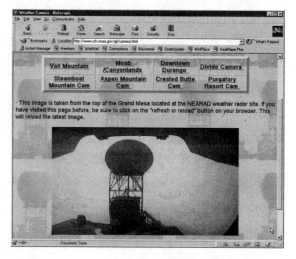

Webcams—Your Window
to the World *(cont.)*

The **US Geological Survey** maintains a Webcam at the Streamflow-Gaging Station along the Verde River in Arizona.

http://www.daztcn.wr.usgs.gov/webcam/cam_09511300.html

Scroll down the Web page to read additional information about the equipment used and how the project was set up.

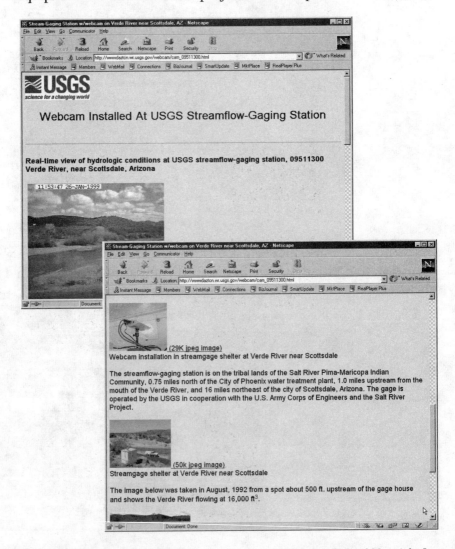

Webcams—Your Window
to the World *(cont.)*

NASA Kennedy Space Center maintains a Web page with a dozen Webcams from various sites. You can watch shuttle and rocket launches, view weather conditions in the area, and see work being completed in the Space Station Processing Facility.

http://www.ksc.nasa.gov/shuttle/countdown/video/

By clicking the hyperlinks, you can find additional information about each of the video feeds, such as the Stardust rocket mission.

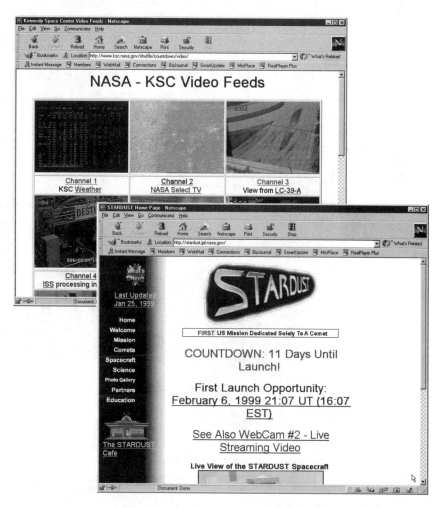

Webcams—Your Window
to the World *(cont.)*

The **Project Galileo** Web site also has reloading images. They are simulated views of the Galileo spacecraft. They are computer generated and are reloaded every five minutes.

http://www.jpl.nasa.gov/galileo/countdown/

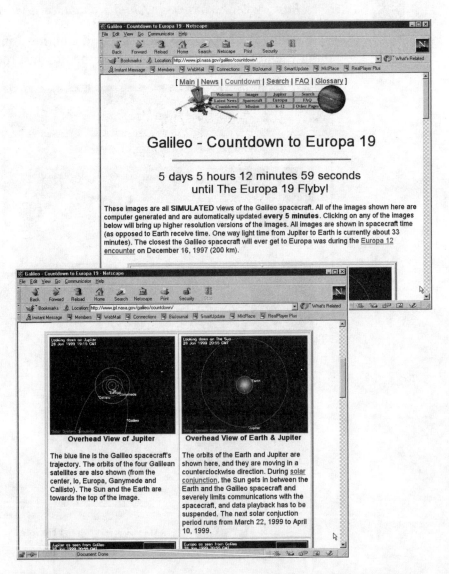

Webcams—Your Window to the World *(cont.)*

Here are some more Web sites where you can find additional Webcams or information about creating one for your classroom.

EarthCam

http://www.earthcam.com/

This Web site is a searchable index to many Webcams around the world.

The WebCam Resource

http://www.webcamresource.com/Regional/

This is another searchable index of Webcams.

WebCam World

http://www.webcamworld.com/

This site contains information about Webcams, new Webcams online, and a searchable index.

North American WebCams

http://gallery.uunet.be/internetpress/star00.htm

This site contains a list of Webcams in North America.

Coastal Imaging Lab—Oregon State University

http://cil-www.oce.orst.edu:8080/

This site maintains Webcams along various coastlines. Click the menu list or the image map to see the Webcams.

WebCam32—Neil Kolban

http://kolban.com/webcam32/

This site has Windows '95+ software to manage a Webcam.

SiteCam—Rearden Technology

http://www.rearden.com/sitecam/default.html

This site has Macintosh software to support sending Webcam images to a Web site.

Netscape Messenger

Messenger is the electronic mail (e-mail) component of the *Netscape Communicator* package. You will use this to exchange e-mail with other Internet users. Once you have set up all of the options in your preferences, you are ready to start sending and receiving e-mail.

In the Starting Out section of this book, you entered your *Netscape* preference options using the Menu Bar.

You can open the *Messenger* program by clicking the **Inbox** button on the floating tool bar.

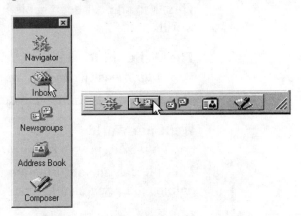

If you have another component of *Communicator* open, you can click the **Inbox** button on the bottom right of the component window.

You can also access *Messenger* from within any other component by clicking the **Messenger** option in the **Communicator** menu.

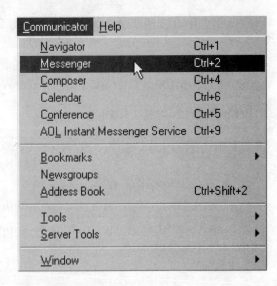

Receiving and Sending E-mail

When you first open *Messenger*, you will see this screen.

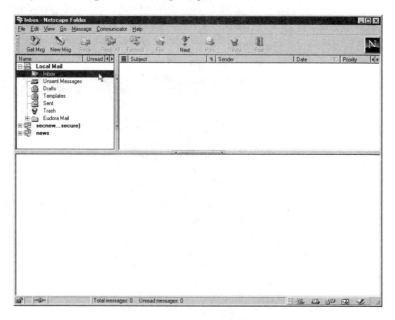

1. Click the *Get Msg* button to retrieve new e-mail messages.

2. Key your password into the blank in the *Password Entry* dialog box.

3. Click the *OK* button.

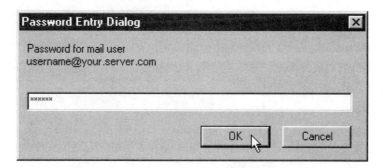

Receiving and Sending E-mail *(cont.)*

You will see this dialog box as your computer connects to your Internet provider and downloads any e-mail you may have.

4. Click ***Inbox***. Your new e-mail messages will appear in the upper right-hand box.

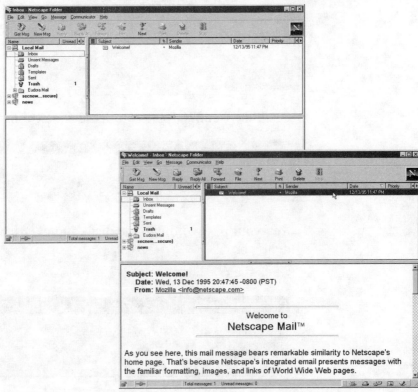

5. Click the e-mail heading. The message will appear in the lower box. Your first e-mail message will be from *Netscape*.

Receiving and Sending E-mail *(cont.)*

6. If you want to answer this e-mail message, you can click the **Reply** button.

The e-mail composition window opens automatically. The **To:** line is filled in with the recipient's e-mail address. The **Subject** line is filled in with "Re:" and then the sender's subject line.

7. You can key in your message to the recipient. The sender's message will automatically appear at the bottom of your reply. You can move your cursor down the screen and delete part of or the entire message. This is helpful if you want to retain part of the message within your reply.

Receiving and Sending E-mail *(cont.)*

8. When you have finished writing your reply, click the ***Send***
button of the Composition window tool bar to send the
e-mail message.

You will also want to write new messages to people whose e-mail
addresses you have.

1. Click the ***New Msg*** button on the *Messenger* tool bar. The
Composition window will open.

2. Enter the recipient's e-mail address in the ***To:*** line.

3. Enter a subject heading in the ***Subject:*** blank.

4. Type your message in the body space.

5. Click the ***Send*** button when you have completed your
message.

Address Book

You can keep a directory of e-mail addresses in the Address Book. You will not have to scroll through all of your e-mail messages to find someone's address.

1. Select ***Address Book*** from the *Communicator* menu.

2. Select ***Personal Address Book***.

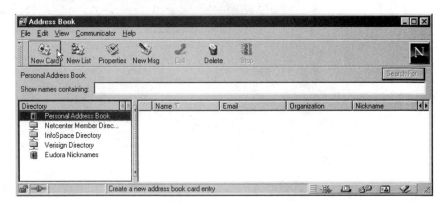

3. Click the ***New Card*** button to create a new entry in your address book.

Address Book *(cont.)*

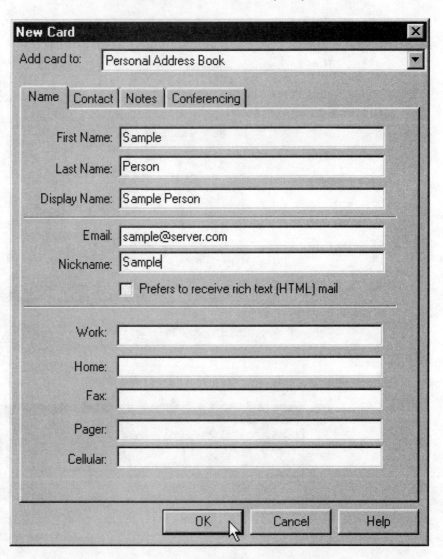

4. Enter the information about this person. You can fill in as little or as much information as you want, but you must fill in an e-mail address and name.

5. Once you have completed entering information, click the **OK** button to return to the Address Book window.

Address Book *(cont.)*

You will now see your address entry listed in the right-hand section of the Address Book window.

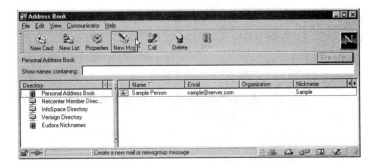

6. To send an e-mail message to this person, click the *New Msg* button on the Address Book tool bar.

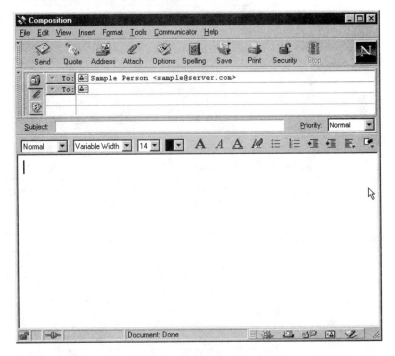

The Composition window will automatically open. The address from the address book will be entered into the *To*: line. You can then enter a Subject line and the body of your message.

Attaching Files to an E-mail Message

You can send other documents, graphics, or program files with an e-mail message.

Note: Keep in mind that the recipient must have a program to view or read whatever file you send. You must be aware that large files will take some time to process through your e-mail server as well as that of the recipient.

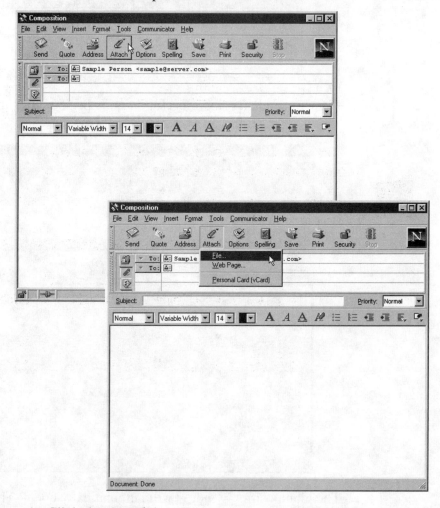

1. Click the *Attach* button on the Composition window tool bar.
2. Select *File* to attach a file to the e-mail message.

Attaching Files to an E-mail Message *(cont.)*

3. Find the file you want to send and click to select it.
4. Click the **Open** button.

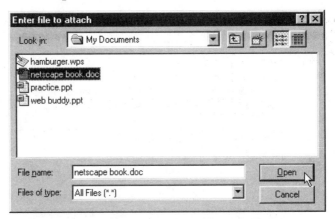

You will see the file listed on the Attachment tab. You can send more than one file attachment with a single e-mail message.

Note: Again, be aware of the collective size of the files you are sending.

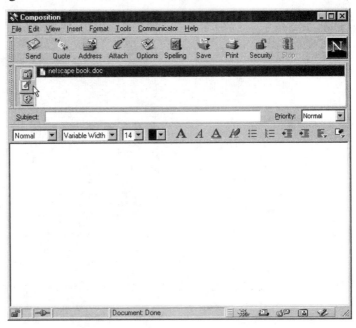

Receiving E-mail with a File Attached

What do you do when you get an e-mail message with a file attached to it? The e-mail message will look similar to this one.

The attached file(s) will be listed at the bottom of the e-mail message.

Click the hyperlink to the file.

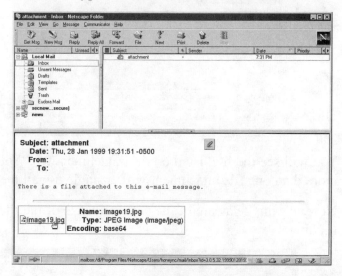

In this case, the file is a graphic. *Navigator* is the associated program to open the file.

By clicking the hyperlink, the instruction is given to open *Navigator* and display the image.

Attaching a Web Page to an E-mail Message

As another option, you can send a copy of a Web page as an attachment to an e-mail message.

Note: Remember, the entire Web page, including graphics, sounds, and multimedia will be sent to the recipient.

1. Select *Web Page* from the *Attach* menu.

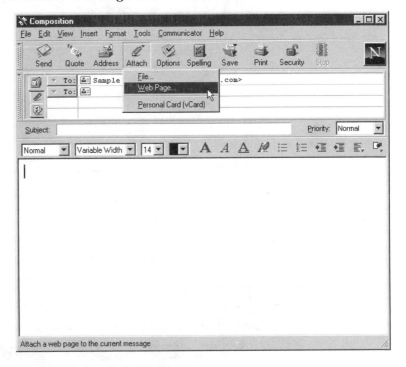

2. Specify the URL of the Web page you want to attach to the e-mail message.

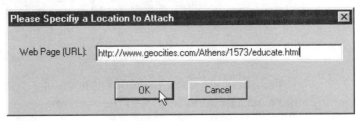

Attaching a Web Page to an E-mail Message *(cont.)*

The attached Web page URL will appear on the Attachment tab.

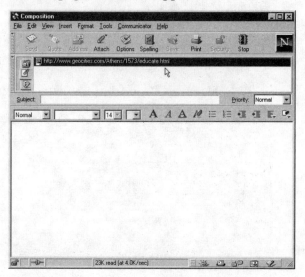

When you set up the Web page to be attached to the e-mail message, it loads into your computer's memory. If there is a large sound or video file attached to the page, it may take a few minutes to download into your computer before you can send it.

3. Once the page has loaded, click *Send* to send the e-mail message. As the Web page is being sent, you will see the progress in the *Sending Message* dialog box.

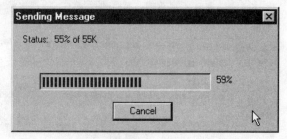

If the file is too large or your connection is too slow, you can click the *Cancel* button to cancel the transfer.

Receiving an E-mail Message with an Attached Web Page

If you receive an e-mail message with a Web page attached, it will look like this:

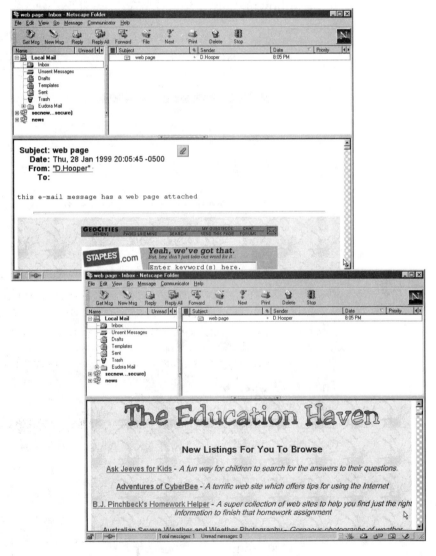

As you scroll down the e-mail message, you will be able to view the entire Web page including graphics, sounds, and videos.

Checking Your Spelling

Messenger has a spelling checker utility that you can use to make sure you have not made a spelling or typing error in your e-mail messages.

In the following message, the word *typed* has been misspelled on purpose.

1. To start to spell check your message, click the *Spelling* button on the Composition tool bar.

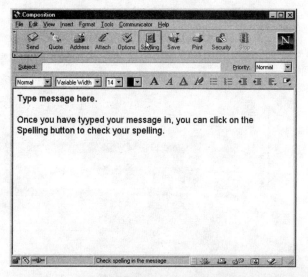

The *Check Spelling* dialog box will appear. It will find the first incorrectly spelled word and suggest possible spelling choices.

2. Select the correct spelling.

3. Click the *Replace* button.

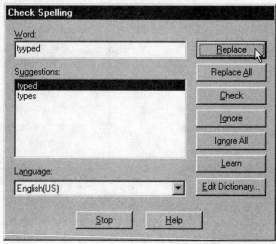

Checking Your Spelling *(cont.)*

The incorrectly spelled word is highlighted in your document so that you can check the context.

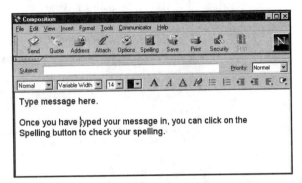

4. When you have finished correcting any errors, click the ***Done*** button.

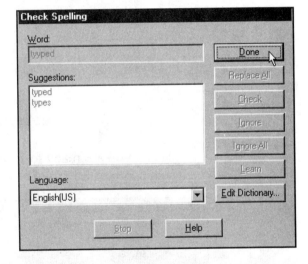

5. Once the message is completely checked, click the ***Send*** button to send the e-mail.

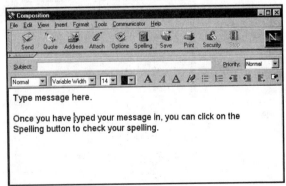

Saving a Draft of an E-mail Message

There may be times when you are working on an e-mail message and need to stop to do something else. You can save the draft, reopen it, and finish it at a later time.

1. Click the *Save* button to save the message.

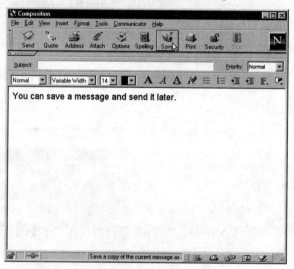

2. When you are ready to work on the e-mail message again, you can find it in the *Drafts* folder.

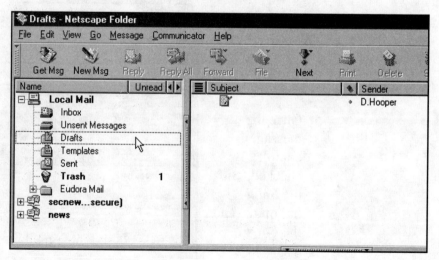

Saving a Draft of an E-mail Message *(cont.)*

3. Select the draft you want to open.

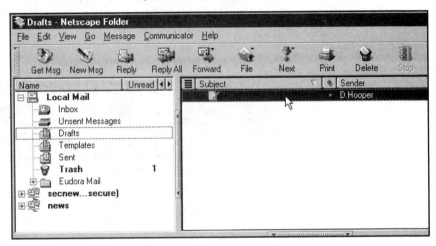

4. Right-click the e-mail listing.

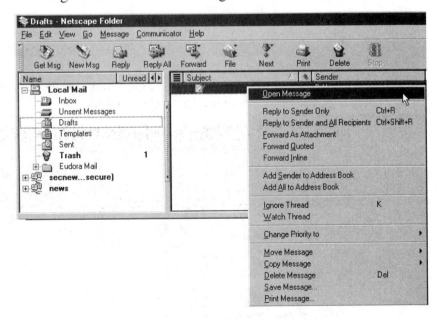

5. Choose ***Open Message*** from the drop-down menu. You can then finish your message and send the e-mail.

Entering Special Characters

If you are sending an e-mail message that needs special characters, there is a *Character Map* option where you will find those characters.

1. Click *Tools* and select *Character Tools*.
2. Click *Insert Special Characters*.

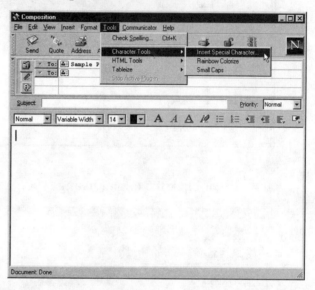

3. Click the character you need to add to your message.

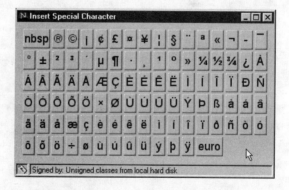

The character will be inserted and the Insert Special Character box will disappear.

Organizing Your E-mail

To bring some order to your e-mail instead of saving it all in your Inbox, you can create additional mail folders and move related messages into them.

1. Select *New Folder* from the *File* drop-down menu.

2. Enter a name for the new mail folder.
3. Click the *OK* button to add the folder to your list.

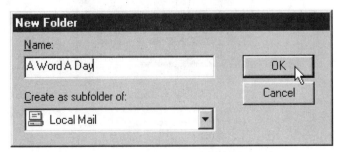

Organizing Your E-mail *(cont.)*

4. Click the e-mail message you want to move. Do not release your mouse button, but drag the message over to the correct folder in your list.

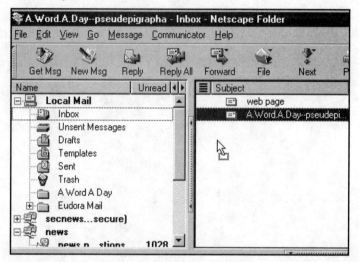

5. Release the mouse button when the cursor is over the folder where you want to place the message.

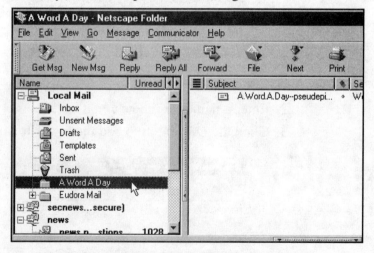

6. To see messages in a folder, click the folder name. Messages will now appear in a list on the right-hand side of the window.

Deleting E-mail Messages

You probably will not want to keep every e-mail message you receive. You will want to delete some periodically.

1. Select the e-mail message you want to delete.

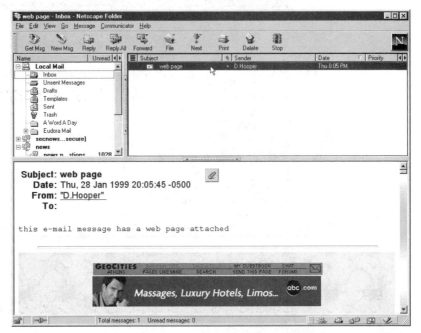

2. Right-click the message you want to delete.

3. Click the **Delete Message** option from the drop-down menu.

This will not permanently delete the message. It will move the message to the **Trash** folder.

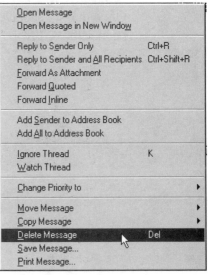

Deleting E-mail Messages *(cont.)*

4. Click the ***Trash*** folder icon to open that folder.

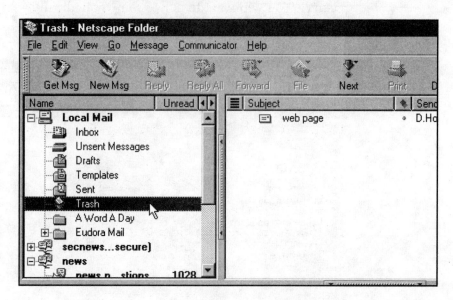

5. To permanently delete a message, select it, right-click the message, and select the ***Delete Message*** option or press the ***Delete*** key on your keyboard.

Once messages have been deleted from the ***Trash*** folder, they have been removed from your computer.

E-mail in the Classroom

Now that you have the ability to send and receive e-mail messages, how do you incorporate that into the curriculum? There are many Web sites that have ideas for using e-mail as part of a classroom activity.

One site is **ePals**. It is located at this URL:

http://www.epals.com/

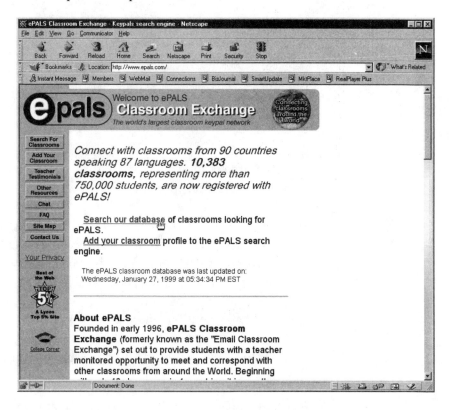

You can search through their database of classrooms from all over the world to find partners for collaborative projects.

1. Click the hyperlink for ***Search for Classrooms***.

E-mail in the Classroom *(cont.)*

The newest additions to the project's list will be located at the bottom of this page.

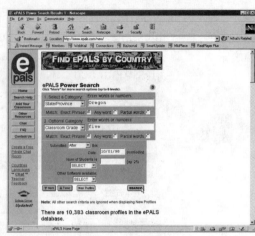

You can also find **ePals** by searching various criteria.

2. Fill in the form with your selections for age, grade, location, etc.

3. Click the *Search* button.

Projects are listed with teacher name, languages, e-mail address, grade levels, student ages, number of students per class, location, and a description of their project.

Here are a few sample project descriptions:

Description: We are currently studying weather and will be studying recycling beginning in April. We would like to communicate with any class that would be interested in sharing information with us on these topics as well as communicating with us in general. I will be using this experience not only as a lesson in technology but in writing, too. We would like to correspond about one time per week.

Description: I am looking for native Spanish speakers, anywhere in the world that would like to communicate via e-mail with some of my students. I teach levels two and three. I would like the communication to alternate languages, one time in English and the next time in Spanish. That way both groups can practice their second language. We are flexible with subject areas, frequency, length, etc.

E-mail in the Classroom *(cont.)*

Description: I have 27 students, 9 boys and 18 girls. I am interested in matching each student with a keypal somewhere in the USA, preferably in another corner of the country. Our school is located in the country, although it is only 20 miles from Portland, Oregon, and 10 miles from the nearest suburb. I would like to correspond with a class that lives in the inner city or a very small town.

You can also create and submit your own project idea.

1. Click *Add your classroom*.

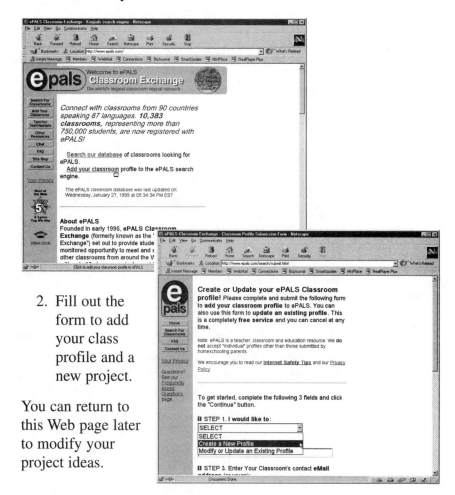

2. Fill out the form to add your class profile and a new project.

You can return to this Web page later to modify your project ideas.

E-mail in the Classroom *(cont.)*

3. Fill in all of the information about your class and include a description of your project.

Note: You might want to participate in a few projects before starting one of your own. Read through several others before creating your own description.

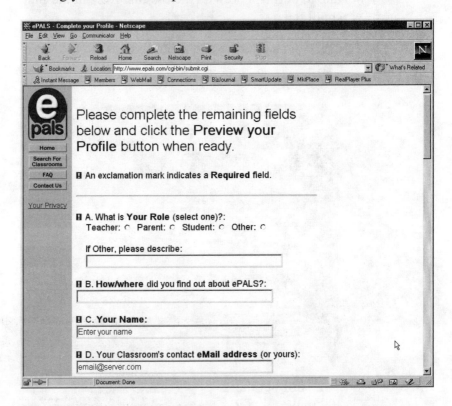

Make sure you practice sending and receiving e-mail before participating in one of these projects. It is important to make sure that everyone has a successful experience with the collaboration.

E-mail in the Classroom *(cont.)*

The Global Schoolhouse maintains a large database of online projects. The projects are located at this URL:

http://www.gsn.org/

1. Click the ***Projects*** button to see current activities.

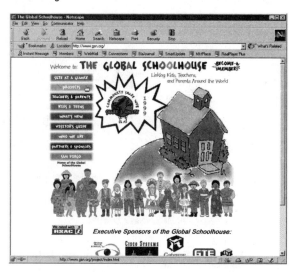

2. Click the banner to go to the ***Projects Registry***. This is where you can search for projects that meet your criteria.

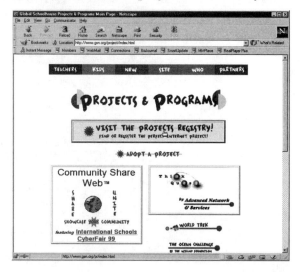

E-mail in the Classroom *(cont.)*

The Global Schoolhouse maintains a registry of current projects as well as an archive of past projects.

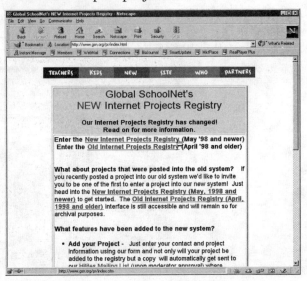

3. Click *Simple Project Search* to find projects.
4. Click *Advanced Project Search* to find projects that meet selected criteria.

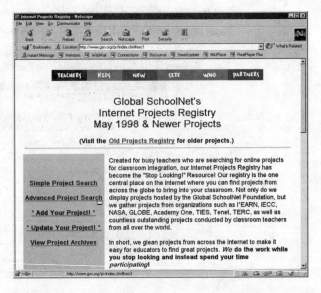

E-mail in the Classroom *(cont.)*

5. Select a ***Curriculum*** area by clicking in the box.

6. Check the ***E-mail*** box to select only those projects that will be carried out via e-mail.

7. Click the ***Submit Search*** button to search the database.

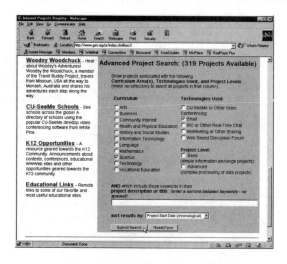

The **Projects Registry** will return a list of projects to you.

8. Click the hypertext link for each project to read more about it. There will be a contact person's e-mail address listed. You can send e-mail to that person in order to participate.

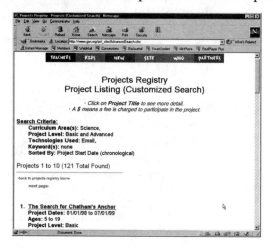

E-mail in the Classroom *(cont.)*

Another Web site that houses online projects is **NickNacks—Telecollaborate**.

They are located at this URL:

http://home.talkcity.com/academydr/nicknacks/

1. Click the ***Enter*** hyperlink to go to the Web site index page.

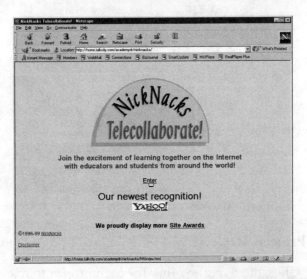

2. You can click the hyperlink ***Find Projects*** or the hyperlink to read ***Examples of Telecollaborations***.

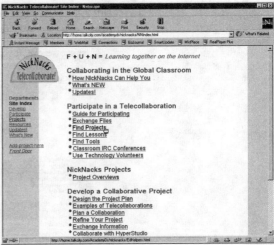

E-mail in the Classroom *(cont.)*

Some projects that have been listed at **NickNacks** include:

Playwriting in the Round

Classes in grades 5-10 collaborated with three classes in the same grade level to write scripts of four mystery plays. Each play consists of four acts, one act written by each of the classes in the script circle. At the conclusion of the project, each class has four original plays for use in other dramatic activities. The activity culminated with an optional IRC (Internet Relay Chart) conference on the dramatic process.

Exchanging Spreadsheets

Grades 2–6 classes exchanged, compiled, and analyzed data on their favorite pets, sports, foods, school subjects, etc.

Once the projects are completed, some of the classes have shared their results with the Web site. For example, there are samples of the spreadsheets and charts created by the classes that participated in the Exchanging Spreadsheets project.

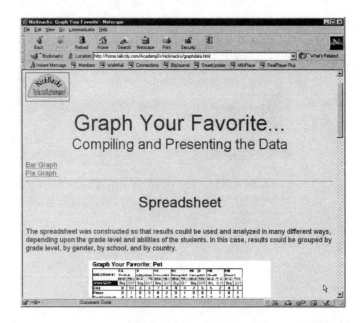

E-mail in the Classroom *(cont.)*

Some Web sites offer you the opportunity to sign up to receive site content and update information. One site that offers this service is **Neuroscience for Kids**. Dr. Eric Chudler maintains this URL:

http://weber.u.washington.edu/~chudler/neurok.html

This site has been created for teachers and students and offers information and activities about the nervous system.

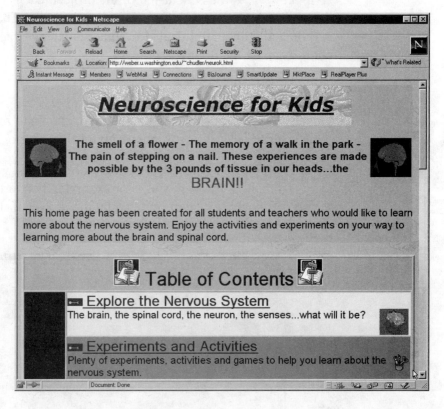

1. Scroll down the Table of Contents to see hypertext links to various topics and activities.

E-mail in the Classroom *(cont.)*

2. Click the *Newsletter* hypertext link.

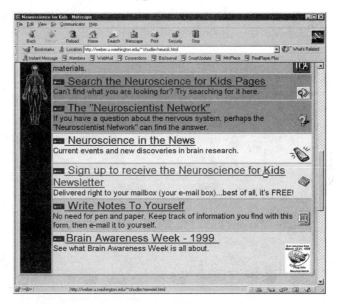

3. To receive the newsletter, click the e-mail hyperlink to send an e-mail message with your e-mail address and a short description of yourself.

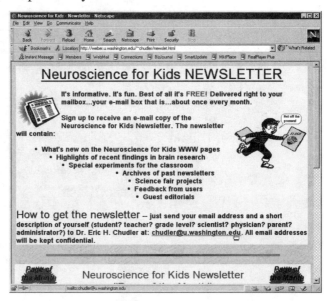

E-mail in the Classroom *(cont.)*

Another Web site which offers a daily e-mail message is **A Word A Day**. You and your students can receive a daily e-mail with a new word and its definition.

It is located at this URL:

http://www.wordsmith.org/awad/

1. Click the hypertext link to subscribe to the newsletter.

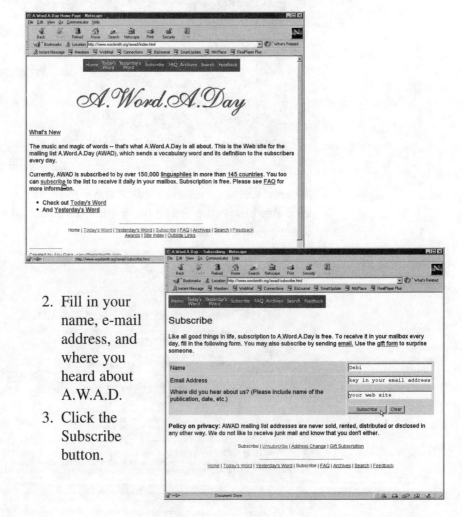

2. Fill in your name, e-mail address, and where you heard about A.W.A.D.

3. Click the Subscribe button.

E-mail in the Classroom *(cont.)*

You will receive an e-mail message confirming your subscription. You will then receive an e-mail message each day with a new word, the definition, etymology, a sentence using the word, and links to a sound file with the pronunciation.

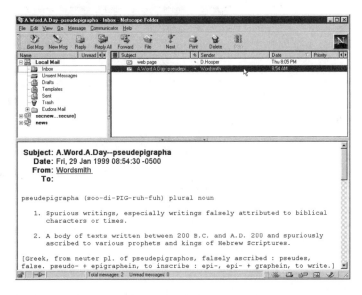

4. Click the hyperlink to hear a pronunciation of the word.

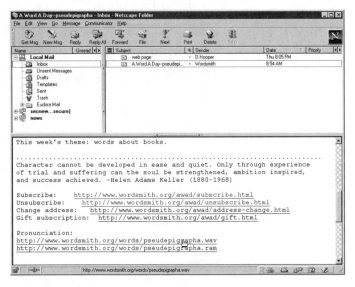

E-mail in the Classroom *(cont.)*

If you do not want to subscribe and receive this in your e-mail every day, you can visit the Web site to see each day's new word.

5. Click the hyperlink to ***Check out Today's Word***.

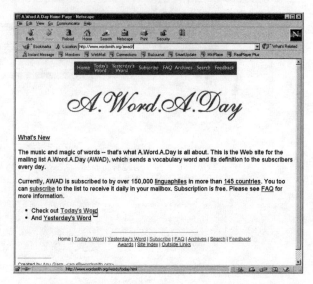

The information about each word is on the Web page.

6. Click the hyperlink for the pronunciation.

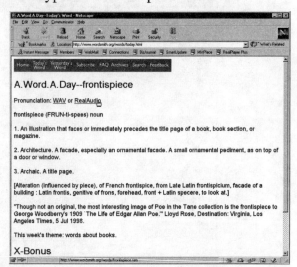

E-mail in the Classroom *(cont.)*

There are also mailing lists to which you can subscribe. You will then receive daily or periodic e-mail messages from other subscribers to the list. Mailing lists or list servers exist for a variety of subjects.

There is a list about using the World Wide Web in education. This is a great place to read how other educators are integrating the Internet into their curriculum. It is also a good forum for posting a message about a problem you might be having and for receiving replies from other educators who may have already encountered and solved that problem.

This mailing list is called **WWWEDU** (pronounced "we do"). Additional information can be found on the Web site at this URL:

http://edweb.gsn.org/wwwedu.html

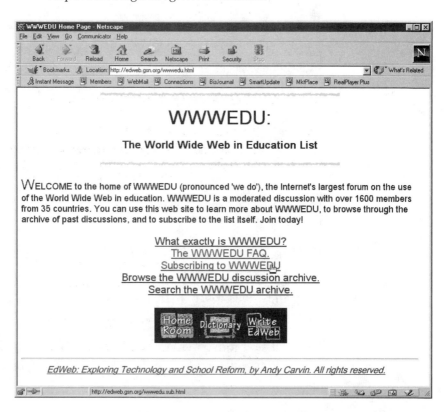

E-mail in the Classroom *(cont.)*

To join **WWWEDU**, you can send a message to

listproc@ready.cpb.org

and in the body of the message, write *subscribe wwwedu your name* and nothing else. You will then be added to the **WWWEDU** list. Be sure to put your name where it says "your name!"

Your e-mail message will look like this:

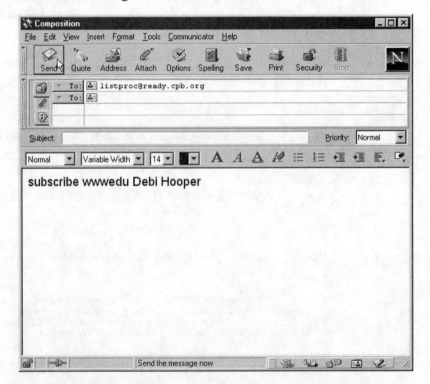

You will receive a welcoming message with information on how to send messages to the list. When you send in a message, it will then be sent to all of the members on the list.

When you first join **WWWEDU**, please post an introduction of yourself to the group and feel free to suggest any discussion topics.

E-mail in the Classroom *(cont.)*

Some of the topics discussed on the list have included the following:

- Discussions about new Web sites
- Filtering software
- Notices about conferences
- Calls for authoring articles
- New releases of teaching materials
- Requests for information
- Requests for software/hardware recommendations
- Information about classroom projects

There are many other e-mail lists. You can use these Web sites to find lists about topics of interest to you and your students.

E-mail Discussion Lists
http://edweb.gsn.org/lists.html

Reference.com—search engine for finding e-mail lists
http://www.reference.com/

Blue Web'n—Library of Learning Sites—Weekly Updates
http://www.kn.pacbell.com/wired/bluewebn/

Catalist—the official list of LISTSERV(r) mailing lists
http://www.lsoft.com/lists/listref.html

Liszt—the mailing list directory
http://www.liszt.com/

NeoSoft—Publicly Accessible Mailing Lists
http://www.neosoft.com/internet/paml/

E-mail Discussion Groups
http://www.webcom.com/impulse/list.html

Newsgroups

Netscape Messenger can also be used to access and participate in newsgroups. Newsgroups are discussion groups about a particular topic or subject. A message sent to a newsgroup is called a "post." A post can be seen by millions of people who choose to read that newsgroup.

You can start the Newsgroup mode in *Messenger* by clicking the button at the bottom right-hand corner of any of the component windows.

Another way to access newsgroups is by selecting the ***Newsgroups*** option from the ***Communicator*** drop-down menu.

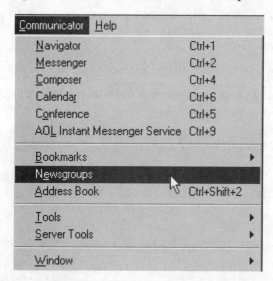

You can also click the ***Newsgroups*** button on the floating tool bar.

Newsgroups that you already subscribe to are listed just below your e-mail boxes.

Newsgroups *(cont.)*

1. The *Netscape* **Netcenter** will appear in the message window as *Messenger* opens.

2. Click the newsgroup listing if you have already subscribed to newsgroups.

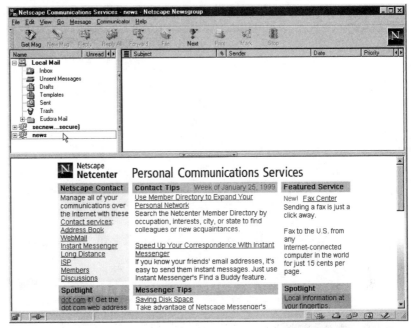

If you have not yet subscribed to any newsgroups, you can add them from the news listing provided by your Internet service provider.

3. Click *Subscribe* in the *File* menu.

Newsgroups *(cont.)*

Your computer will check the listings of all possible newsgroups available to which you can subscribe. There are hundreds of possible groups.

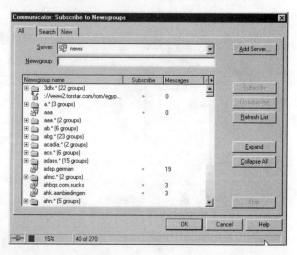

You can either browse the list, key in a newsgroup name, or search for groups that match keywords.

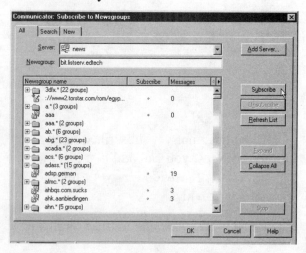

4. If you know the name of the newsgroup to which you want to subscribe, key the name into the blank and click the ***Subscribe*** button.

Newsgroups *(cont.)*

5. To search for certain types of newsgroups, click the ***Search*** tab.

6. Enter the keyword(s).

7. Click the ***Search Now*** button.

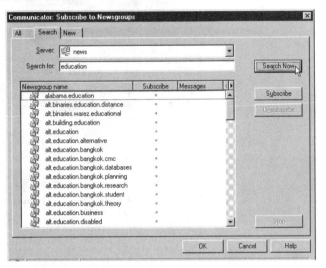

8. Once you select a newsgroup you would like to read, click the ***Subscribe*** button.

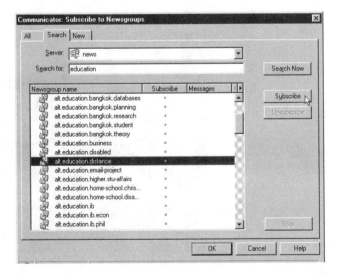

Newsgroups *(cont.)*

9. Once you have subscribed to several newsgroups, you can click the *News* listing. You will see the number of unread messages appear.

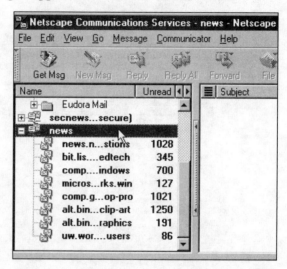

10. Select the newsgroup you want to read. If there are more than 500 messages (or the number you set in your preferences), then you will see this dialog box.

11. You can choose whether to download all of the available messages or just 500.

12. You can change the limit to another number by keying in that number.

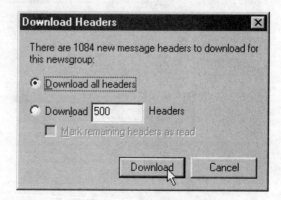

Newsgroups *(cont.)*

A newsgroup to which you may want to subscribe is the
EDTECH group. It is offered as a mailing list or as a newsgroup.

You can find information about the **EDTECH** list and newsgroup
at this URL:

http://h-net2.msu.edu/~edweb/

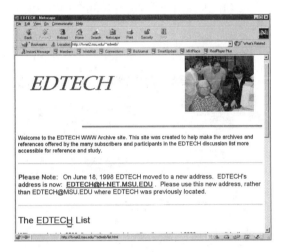

The newsgroup name for
the **EDTECH** group is
bit.listserv.edtech.

The conversations in this
newsgroup are about using
technology in the class-
room. There are discus-
sions about hardware, software, and curriculum.

13. To access the mes-
    sages in a newsgroup,
    click that listing.

Newsgroups *(cont.)*

As the messages are downloading, you will see the status at the bottom of the *Messenger* window.

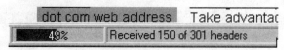

The message list will appear in the upper right-hand block of the *Messenger* window.

14. Click a message header to read it.

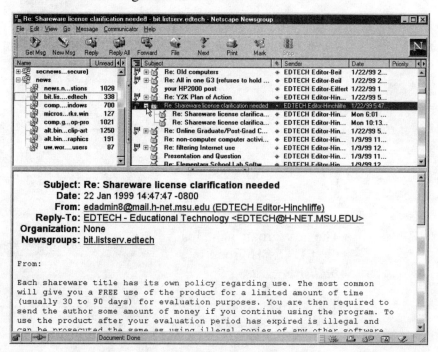

If there are more messages for a topic, there will be a + sign to the left of the main header.

15. Click the + sign to see the rest of the messages for that topic or thread.

Newsgroups *(cont.)*

16. If you want to reply to a message, click the **Reply** button on the tool bar.

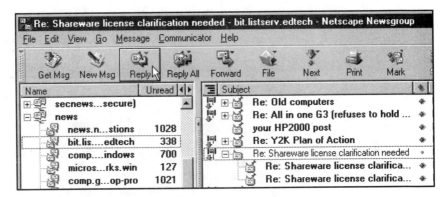

The reply will go to the newsgroup instead of just to the individual who posted the message.

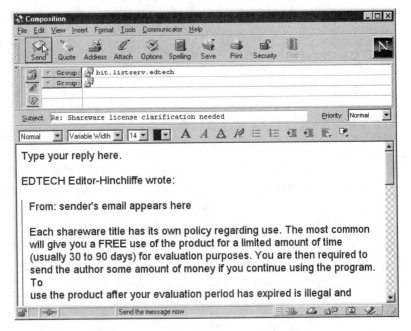

You will use the Composition utility to type your reply as if you were sending an e-mail message.

Newsgroups *(cont.)*

Once you have read the messages you want to read, you can mark the other messages as "read." The next time you access the newsgroup, you will download all new messages.

17. To mark messages as read, select **Mark** from the **Message** drop-down menu.

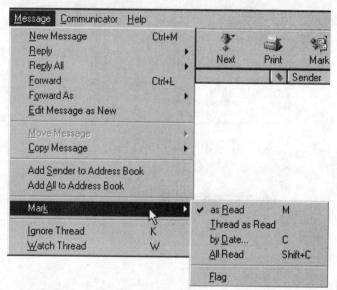

18. Then select whether to mark a **Thread** (or topic) **as Read** or to mark **All Read**.

19. To unsubscribe from a newsgroup, click it and press the **Delete** key on your keyboard. Click **OK** when asked if you are sure you want to unsubscribe.

To find additional descriptions of newsgroups, you can visit these Web sites.

BizProWeb—Education Newsgroup List
http://www.bizproweb.com/pages/newsgroups/education.html

Liszt's Usenet Newsgroup Directory
http://www.liszt.com/news/

Composing Web Pages

Web pages are created with instructions called HTML or HyperText Markup Language. This programming language was developed so that all computers and browser formats can read it. Whether you have a Windows-based computer or a Macintosh, you will be able to view the same Web pages.

Creating your own Web pages can be one way to improve your school-to-home connection. Parents who have access to the World Wide Web can read your Web pages and find out what is happening in your classroom. Student projects, field trips, on-going class activities, book reviews, and just about any other project can be made into a Web page and shared with other teachers, classes, and parents.

If your school has its own Web server, you can find out how to post your Web pages to it. You will probably need to check with whomever is your Webmaster or technology person who maintains your network.

If your school does not have its own Web server on-site, there are several Web sites that allow you to have free Web space to publish your own Web pages. These sites make their money from advertisers who pay to have their banner advertisements appear on your Web pages. Some of these sites allow you to pay a monthly fee instead of putting the advertising banners on your page.

Here are some sites with which you can start.

Geocities
http://www.geocities.com

Fortune City
http://www2.fortunecity.com/

Tripod
http://www.tripod.com

Free Sites Network
http://www.fsn.net/

Angelfire
http://www.angelfire.com/

Talk City
http://home.talkcity.com/

Composing Web Pages *(cont.)*

Once you visit those sites and decide to start your own Web site, you need to plan what you are going to put in it. Plan carefully. If you design a basic outline of your Web site, you can easily add to it. Otherwise you may wind up with a bunch of Web pages floating up in Cyberspace in no particular order.

Here is a brainstorming idea for a classroom Web site.

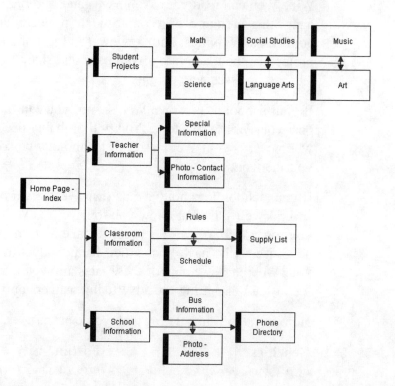

Your home page should be an index to the rest of the Web site. You can direct visitors to the main headings and then include more specific ideas within those groupings.

If you would like more detailed information about planning a Web site and HTML programming, check out a book from Teacher Created Materials, *A Beginner's Guide to Creating Web Pages for School or Classroom.*

Composing Web Pages *(cont.)*

Before creating any Web pages, you should set up a folder on your hard drive in which to keep your Web pages and any other files organized. You may just want to name this folder *Webpages*. Your entire HTML files, graphics, or multimedia files should be saved · to this folder.

To create your Web pages using *Netscape Communicator*'s components, you need to start by opening *Netscape Composer*. You can do this in several ways.

You can click the **Composer** button on the bottom right of any *Netscape* component window.

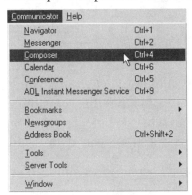

Another method would be to select **Composer** from the **Communicator** menu in any of the components.

You can also click the **Composer** button on the floating tool bar.

To show how *Netscape Composer* works, we will be looking at sample Web pages. These illustrate how you can post information about a class field trip. You will see samples of just a few of the HTML tricks available. This should give you a starting point for creating simple Web pages of your own.

To follow along with the instructions, select the **Sample Field Trip** Web pages from the CD that accompanies this book.

Composing Web Pages *(cont.)*

This set of sample Web pages represents a school field trip to Washington, D.C. There are photographs and captions throughout the pages. Each of the pages has HTML applications that you can use.

The first process before starting a Web page project is to set up a plan. This is the basic plan for the Field Trip Web pages.

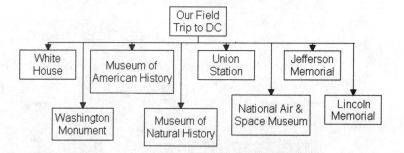

An actual field trip to Washington, D.C. would certainly have more headings for places visited, but this is a simple project to give you some ideas about what you can do. As long as you have space enough to hold your files, you can always add more.

The introductory page has a heading, a graphic, and links to the other Web pages.

If you want to look at the HTML coding, you can view the source code for the sample project.

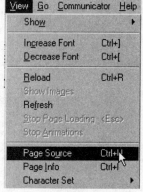

1. Click *View*.
2. Click *Page Source*.

You will see a separate window open with text instructions in it. Look at the middle section to get an idea of the instructions that make this page look the way that it does.

Composing Web Pages *(cont.)*

The body of the page has instructions such as these:

```
<body>
<center>
<h1>
<font color="#000000">Our Field Trip to</font></h1></center>
<center>
<h1>
<font color="#000000">Washington, D.C.</font></h1></center>
<center>
<p><br><img SRC="Dc508.jpg" ALT="Morning Glories"
height=274 width=400></center>
<p>We visited many of the museums and landmarks in our
nation's capital.
<br>Click the links below to see some of our photos.
<p><a href="whitehouse.html">White House</a>
<br><a href="wash-mon.html">Washington Monument</a>
<br><a href="am-hist.html">Museum of American History</a>
<br><a href="nat-hist.html">Museum of Natural History</a>
<br><a href="union.html">Union Station</a>
<br><a href="air-space.html">National Air &amp; Space
Museum</a>
<br><a href="jefferson.html">Jefferson Memorial</a>
<br><a href="lincoln.html">Lincoln Memorial</a>
</body>
```

There are two heading lines at the top of the page.

There is a graphic of flowers.

Then there is text followed by a list of hypertext links to the other pages.

This is a very simple Web page. *Composer* writes all of these instructions for you as you select various options. Here is how that page was created.

Creating a Centered Heading

1. Key in the text for your heading.

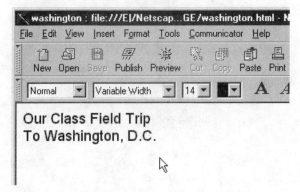

2. Use your mouse to highlight or block the text.

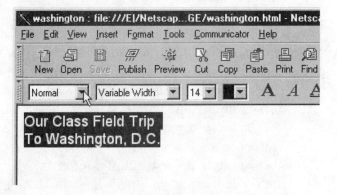

3. Click the drop-down menu that says *Normal*. Select *Heading 1*.

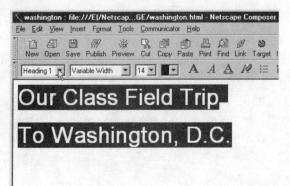

Creating a Centered Heading *(cont.)*

4. Click *Format*.

5. Select *Align*.

6. Click *Center* to center the heading.

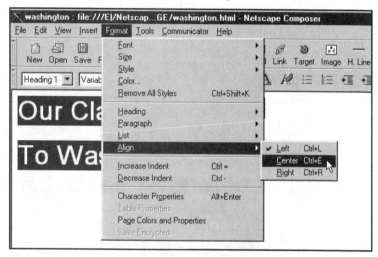

7. You can also click the alignment button on the tool bar and select the button for centering.

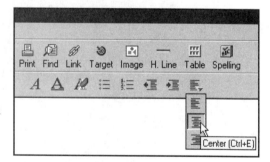

Your heading is now centered at the top of the window.

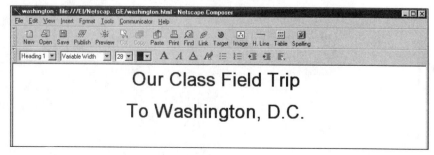

Inserting a Graphic Image

1. Click the *Image* button on the Button Bar.

2. Click the *Choose File* button on the *Image Properties* dialog box.

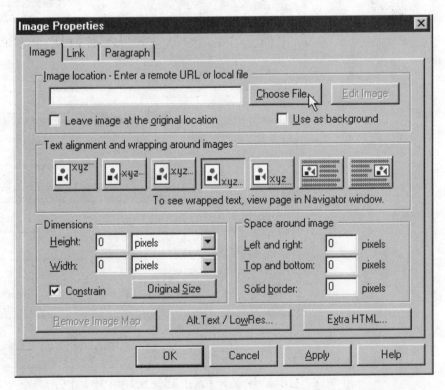

Inserting a Graphic Image *(cont.)*

3. Select the image file from your Web page folder.

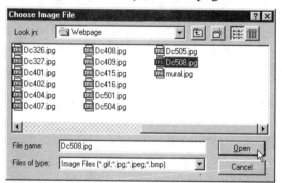

 Note: You should have put all of your graphics in this folder before starting to create the Web pages.

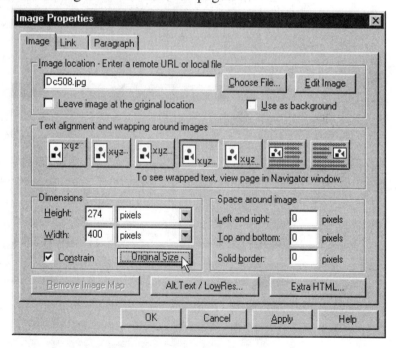

4. Click the ***Original Size*** button to insert the graphic size into your HTML document.

5. Click the ***Alt. Text/LowRes*** button to insert a text description of your graphic image.

Inserting a Graphic Image *(cont.)*

Some browser software will not view graphics, and some people have slow Internet connection speeds so they turn off graphic viewing. By inserting a text description of each image, you are providing those Internet users with an idea of what each image is.

6. Enter a simple description of the image and then click the *OK* button.

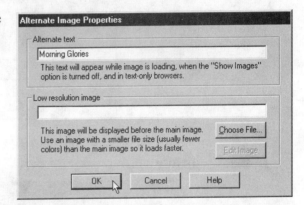

7. Click the *OK* button on the *Image Properties* dialog box.

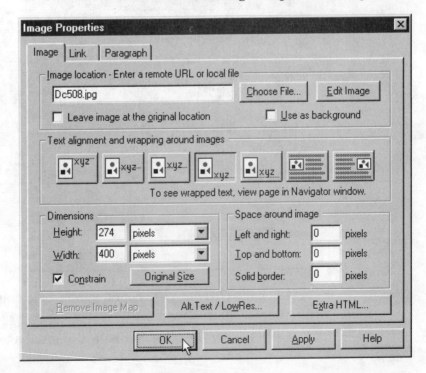

Inserting a Graphic Image *(cont.)*

Your graphic image is now located just under the heading. If it is aligned to the left, you can click to select it and center it as you centered the heading.

The rest of this page is keyed in as plain text. Once the list is keyed in, it can then be set up as hypertext links.

Creating a Hypertext Link

1. Use your mouse to highlight or block the text.

White House
Washington Monument
Museum of American History
Museum of Natural History
Union Station

Creating a Hypertext Link *(cont.)*

2. Click the *Link* button on the Button Bar.

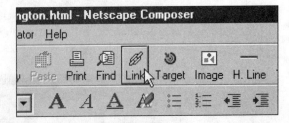

Key in the name of the Web page to which you want this link to refer. You can also use the *Choose File* button to browse and find the Web page. This can be a Web page in your folder or a Web page URL from somewhere else on the World Wide Web.

Note: Remember to keep all of your Web pages within one folder.

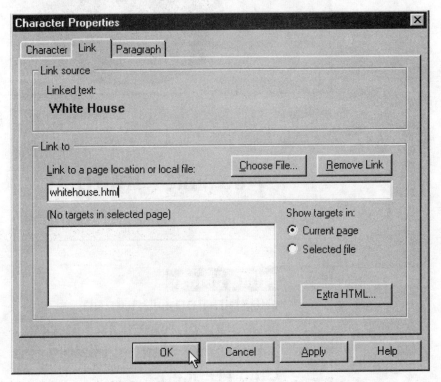

Creating a Hypertext Link *(cont.)*

Your hypertext links will appear in a different text color (blue) and will be underlined. This is the default setting for Web pages. You can change this later if you choose.

Saving Your Web Page

You should save your Web page often while you are working on it. Click the **Save** button and the **Save As** dialog box will appear. Give the page a name and click **Save**.

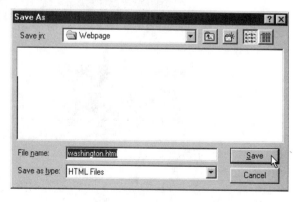

Saving Your Web Page *(cont.)*

As you browse through the sample Web pages, you will see more techniques. These are all simple techniques that you can easily do on your own pages.

The **White House** and **Washington Monument** Web pages are very simple. There is a heading, a graphic image, and a hypertext link back to the main index page. You should always provide visitors to your pages a way back to the main page.

The **Museum of American History** Web page has more graphic images and more text. The images are not centered as on the first pages. You will also see at the bottom of the Web page a hypertext link that allows visitors to return to the index page.

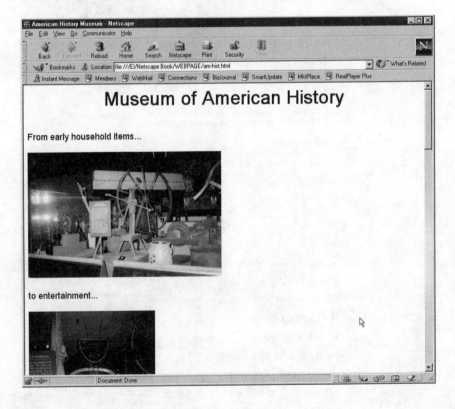

Aligning Text

The Web page for the **Museum of Natural History** uses a different technique for aligning text. When inserting an image, you can decide to align text in a variety of ways. This centers the text alongside the image.

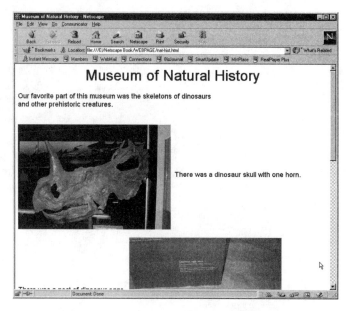

To center the text, click the centering button in the *Image Properties* dialog box.

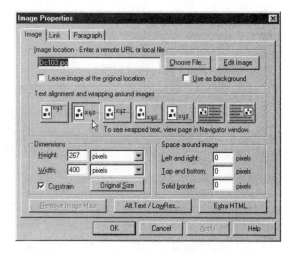

Image Hyperlink

The **Union Station** Web page uses a small graphic image near the bottom of the Web page as a hyperlink to a larger graphic.

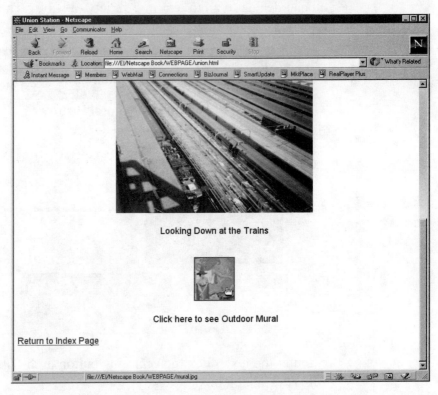

1. In *Composer*, select the image that will be used as a hyperlink.

Click here to see Outdoor Mural

Image Hyperlink *(cont.)*

2. Click the *Link* button on the Button Bar.

3. Enter the Web page URL or a link to another image file in the *Link to* blank of the *Image Properties* dialog box.

This link takes the user to a graphic image.

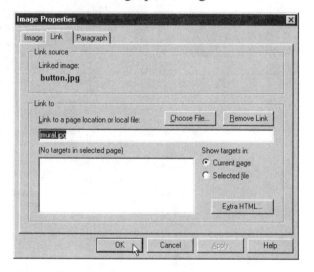

If the link takes users to another graphic image, you should make sure they know how to click the *Back* button of their browser to return to the original Web page.

Page and Text Color

The **Air & Space Museum** Web page adds three more processes. There is a background color, a text color other than black and white, and also a table to organize the graphic images.

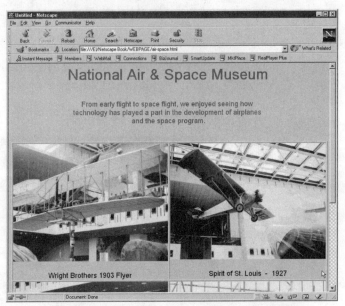

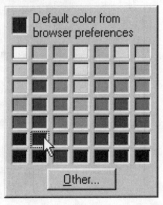

1. To select a font color, click the *Font Color* drop-down button.

2. Once you see the color palette, select the font color of your choice. You can also click the *Other* button and customize your own color.

Page and Text Color *(cont.)*

1. To change the background color of the Web page, select the
   Page Colors and Properties option from the ***Format*** drop-
   down menu.

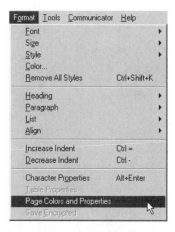

2. Select the ***Colors and Background*** tab in the ***Page
   Properties*** dialog box.

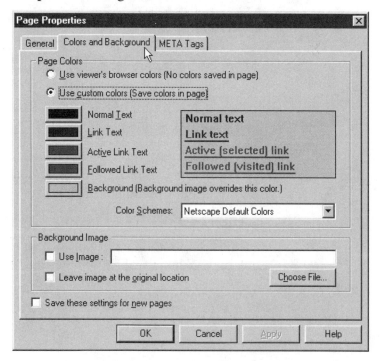

Page and Text Color *(cont.)*

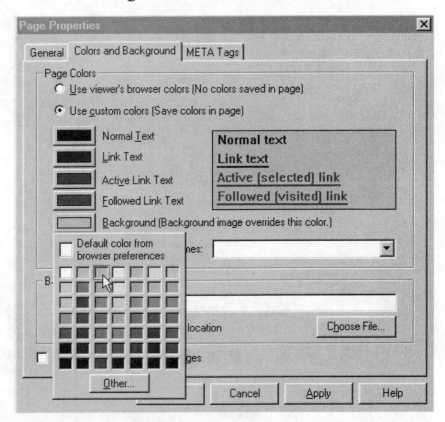

3. To change any of the color options, click the button and then select a color from the palette.

Note: If you use a background image, it will override the color choice. It is still a good idea to use a complementary background color for those users who do not load images.

4. Click the ***Apply*** button to view the color change on your Web page.

5. Click the ***OK*** button when you are finished.

Tables

You should be sure to plan ahead before you create a table to organize images or information. You will need to know how many cells, or spaces, to include in your table. You should also decide if you want the table background to be the same as the Web page background. You may choose to have a different color or a background image.

1. Click the *Table* button on the Button Bar.

2. For the sample page, there are two rows and two columns. The table is aligned in the center of the Web page. The other options are left as the default, or normal, choices. Click the *Apply* button and then *Close*.

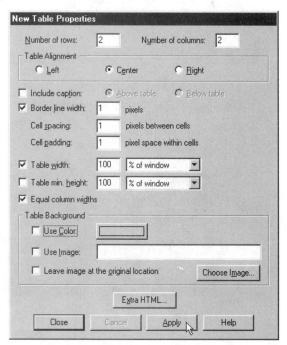

Tables *(cont.)*

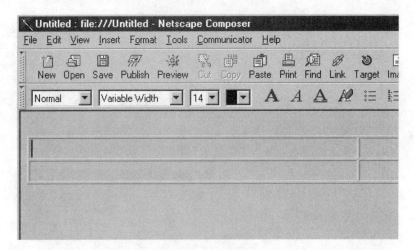

3. Position your cursor within the table cell and enter any information or images you want.

In this page, an image and caption are inserted into each cell. The table is used to align each pair of images next to each other.

You can also choose to have no pixel borders around the table cells or within each cell. You will then have an invisible table in which to organize text or numbers or images.

You can also use a table on your classroom Web site as a way of posting your classroom schedule.

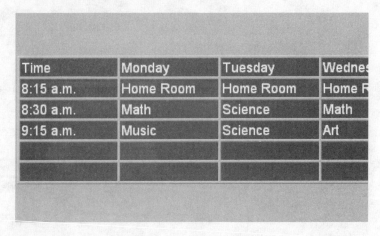

Time	Monday	Tuesday	Wednes
8:15 a.m.	Home Room	Home Room	Home R
8:30 a.m.	Math	Science	Math
9:15 a.m.	Music	Science	Art

Background Images

The **Jefferson Memorial** Web page has a background image. It is a border image with color on the left.

1. Select ***Page Colors and Properties*** from the ***Format*** drop-down menu.

2. Select the background image for the page.

This image should be in the same folder as the Web page and any other graphics.

3. Click to put a check mark next to ***Use Image***.

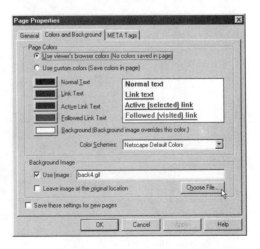

Target Location

The **Lincoln Memorial** Web page makes use of *target* locations within a Web page. This technique is useful if you have a long document on one Web page, and you need to have links to parts of that document.

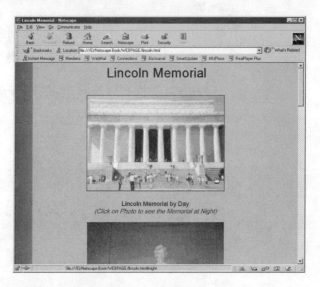

In this case, the targets are the daytime and nighttime photographs of the Lincoln Memorial.

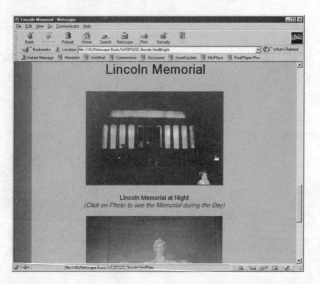

Target Location *(cont.)*

The first step is to designate the targets in your Web page. In this case, the headings for the Lincoln Memorial are the two targets. If you scroll down the entire Web page, you will see that there are two sets of photographs with headings on the one Web page.

1. Position your cursor right before the item you want to make the target.
2. Click the **Target** button.

3. Enter a name for the target in the **Target Properties** dialog box.

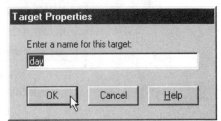

4. Click the **OK** button.

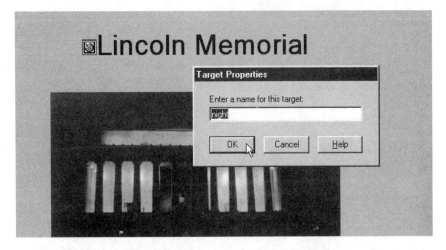

Create all of the targets first. The target next to this heading is named "night."

Target Location *(cont.)*

5. You then select the image or text for the hyperlink. On this Web page, the nighttime photo is selected and is a hyperlink to take the user back to the daytime photo.

6. Then click the ***Link*** button on the Button Bar.

7. Click the ***Link*** tab on the ***Image Properties*** dialog box. The two targets are listed in this dialog box.

8. Select the correct target.

9. Click the ***OK*** button.

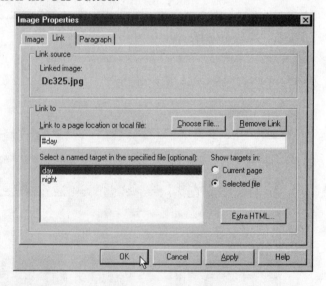

Repeat this process for other links and targets. The Web page will then allow users to quickly browse through a large document. You can use this technique to show before and after photographs of classroom activities or student projects.

Creating a New Web Page

When you complete one Web page and are ready to start a new page, you can click the *New* button on *Composer's* Button Bar.

You will see the ***Create New Page*** dialog box. If you select ***Blank Page***, you will open another blank window in *Composer*. You can then create additional Web pages.

If you select ***From Template***, you will see another dialog box.

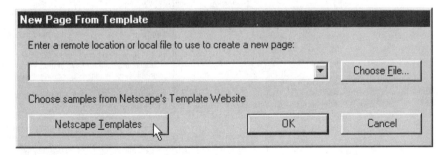

You can click the ***Netscape Templates*** button and see templates that you can personalize.

Creating a New Web Page *(cont.)*

You can also select to use the *Page Wizard*.

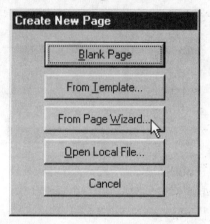

When you click the ***From Page Wizard*** button, a *Navigator* window will open, and you will automatically be taken to this online Web Page Wizard (or creator).

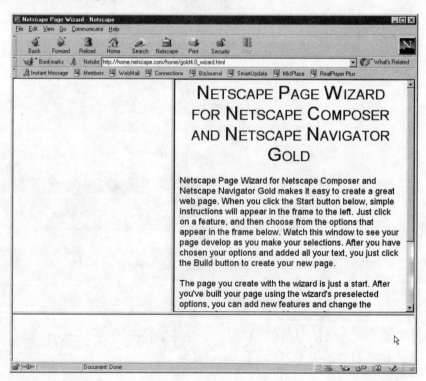

Creating a New Web Page *(cont.)*

Follow the simple online directions to create your own Web page.

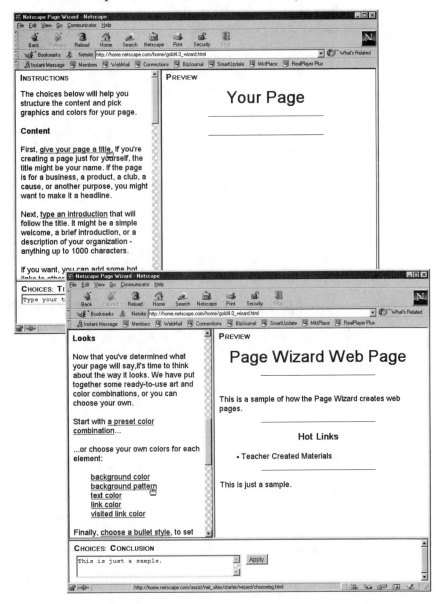

As you enter information, you will see the right-hand side view change to show you how the Web page will look.

Creating a New Web Page *(cont.)*

When you finish creating the Web page, you can click the ***Build*** button at the bottom of the instruction screen. Your Web page will be created, and you can then save it to your hard drive.

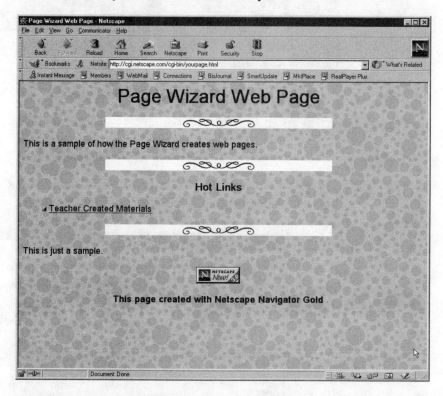

Once you save the Web page, you can publish it to another remote site online.

This is a quick way to create Web pages with lessons and hyperlinks to Web pages for your students to visit. You can key in the topic or a question at the beginning, then list the Web sites you want them to visit under the Hot Links. You can conclude the Web page with a final reminder of the main topic of your assignment.

Publishing Web Pages

Once you have finished creating your Web pages, you will want to publish or post them somewhere. If you are publishing them to your school's Web site, you will need to get specific directions from the Webmaster or network manager at school. If you are publishing them to another location, you can enter the information for that Web site, and *Composer* will upload (move your files to that remote location) for you.

1. Click the ***Publish*** button on *Composer's* Button Bar.

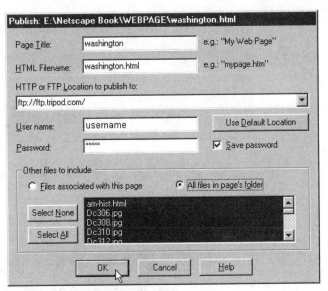

2. Fill in the information for the Web site where you will be uploading your Web pages.

3. Select the option to upload all of the files in this page's folder. This will upload all of the files at one time.

Publishing Web Pages *(cont.)*

You may get a message advising you that references to your links are set on your hard disk. As long as you know the file references are correct, click the *OK* button.

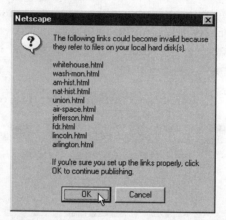

As the files are being uploaded, you will see this status dialog box.

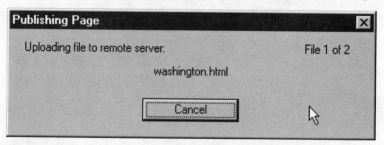

If you designated a Web site URL in the preferences where you would like to view your Web pages, you will see this confirmation when the upload is complete. If you want to view the Web page online, click the *OK* button.

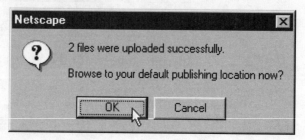

Conferencing in Cyberspace

Netscape Communicator has another utility which will allow you to set up conferences with people all over the world. It is called *Conference*. To set up a conference with others, they need to have the software installed on their computers, as well. Then you can chat, talk via microphone, share files, browse the Web together, and view graphics on the Whiteboard.

1. To start *Conference*, select **Conference** from the **Communicator** drop-down menu.

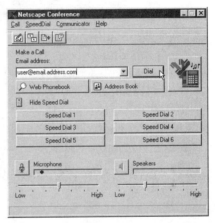

The main *Conference* screen looks like the following.

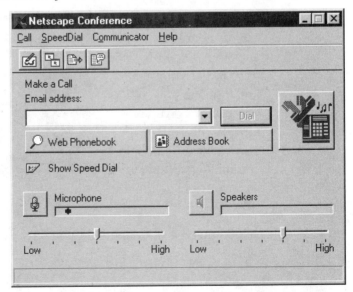

Setting Up a Conference

Before you start to use *Conference*, you will need to set up several options through the Setup Wizard.

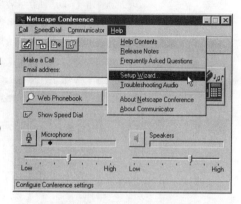

1. Select **Setup Wizard** from *Conference's* **Help** drop-down menu.

2. Click **Next** until you reach this dialog box. You will use it to set up your "Business Card" so that other users will know you and contact you. Your name (or a chat handle) and your e-mail address should be entered.

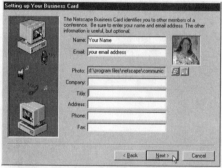

3. Continue to click **Next** as you answer the questions. You may not want to list your name in the phone book. If you want to give your identity information only to specific people, you may want to remove the check mark.

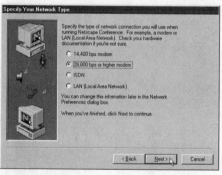

4. Select the type of connection you have and click the **Next** button.

Contacting Other Users

Once you have *Conference* set up, you can contact other users. If you know their e-mail address, key it in and click the **Dial** button to contact them.

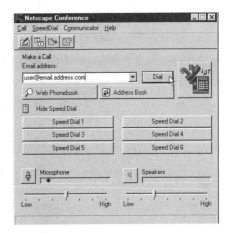

If you want to find other users who might be online, click the **Web Phonebook** button. This will take you to a Web site that has *Conference* users listed.

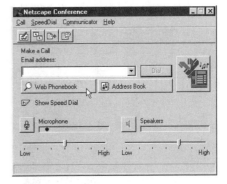

Select a letter to see chat handles or names beginning with that letter. You can also search by name, e-mail address, or location.

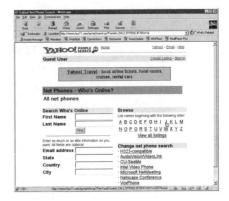

Contacting Other Users *(cont.)*

You can set Speed Dial addresses for the people you dial most often. This is a good idea when setting up other classrooms for your students to contact.

1. Click *Show Speed Dial* if it is not already showing.
2. Click a *Speed Dial* button to set the options.

3. Fill in the information for the user that you want to program on your Speed Dial and click the *OK* button.

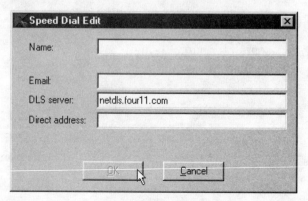

Using the Whiteboard

The Whiteboard is a drawing board that allows you and the other person in your conference to see and write on a diagram, graphic image, or drawing.

1. Click the ***Whiteboard*** button on the ***Conference*** Button Bar.

This will open a drawing board much like the simple draw programs that come as part of your normal operating system.

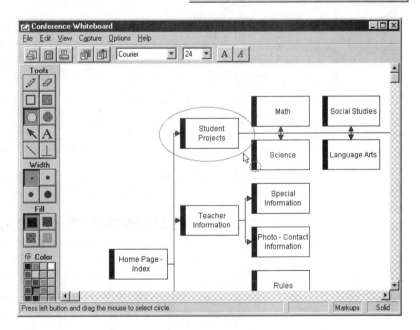

2. You can copy and paste diagrams into the drawing window and use the tools to write, draw, or point out certain parts of the diagram.

File Sharing

You can choose to send files to another user through this program.

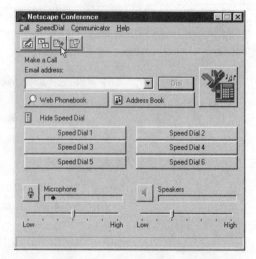

1. Click the *File Transfer* button on the Button Bar.

2. Click the *Open File* button to select which files to send. They will be listed in this box. Then click the *Send* button on the Button Bar.

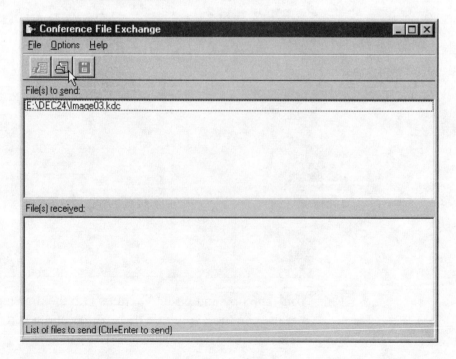

Conference Chatting

You can chat in *Conference* by typing or by microphone.

1. Click the ***Chat*** button.

Messages are typed in the lower window. Each user can read all of the messages. You can also paste a block of text in the window, press ***Ctrl*** and ***Enter***, and send it to the other user.

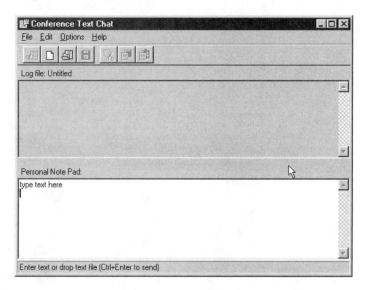

Finding Answers to Your Questions

There are several ways to find answers to questions you may have about using *Netscape Communicator* and all of its components.

The first place to look is the **Unofficial FAQ** (Frequently Asked Questions) Web site. This site archives the answers to questions that many users have asked. Before calling someone or posting a message to a newsgroup, you may want to see if someone else has had the same problem that you are experiencing.

The URL for **The Netscape Unofficial FAQ** Web site is:

http://www.uFAQ.org/

Find the version of *Netscape Communicator* that you are using. Click the link to your corresponding version to see the answers to many questions.

Another way to find answers is to ask someone. If you click the *NUGgies* link, you will go to the **Netscape** Web page about newsgroups to which you can subscribe.

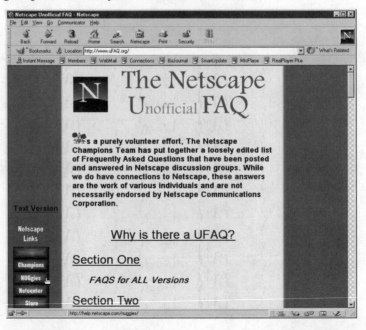

Finding Answers to Your Questions *(cont.)*

The **Netscape Navigator User Group** Web page is at the URL:

http://help.netscape.com/nuggies/navigator.html

There are hyperlinks to subscribe to several different newsgroups.

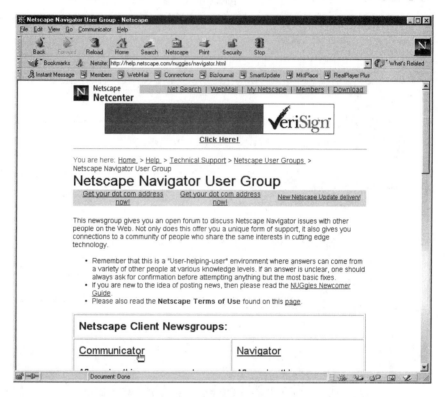

You must be using a newsgroup reader (such as *Netscape Messenger*) to read secure newsgroups. If you click the hyperlinks to those newsgroups, you will automatically subscribe to the groups.

Glossary

Bookmark (Favorite)—A way to store a Web address (URL) without having to write it down to remember it.

Browser—The program that allows you to access and read hypertext documents on the network or on the World Wide Web.

Cache—An area in memory or on your hard disk where copies of frequently accessed web pages and graphics are stored for quick retrieval.

Download—To save a file or web page from the Internet or a network file server to your computer's hard disk or a floppy disk.

E-mail (Electronic Mail)—A system for sending and receiving text messages and attached files between locations via the computer.

FAQ—(Frequently Asked Questions) A web page found at many web sites which provides answers to most questions you may have about that web site.

Favorite—see Bookmark

Frame—A divided section of a web page.

History—A stored list of web sites visited by your computer. This list is kept for a specified number of days.

HTML—HyperText Markup Language—The coding language used to create hypertext documents for use on the World Wide Web.

HTTP—HyperText Transfer Protocol—The process for moving hypertext files across the Internet.

Internet—The collection of over 60,000 inter-connected networks.

Glossary *(cont.)*

Mailing list—A list to which you can send e-mail and it will automatically be forwarded to all members of the list group.

Newsgroup—A discussion group about a particular topic or subject.

Scrolling—Using your mouse or arrow keys to navigate up and down a web page.

Search engine—A web site which offers searching capabilities for you to find links to various web sites that meet your search criteria.

Subscribe—Signing up for a mailing list or newsgroup.

Template—A sample web page that you can edit to easily create your own web page.

Thread—All the messages in a mailing list or newsgroup which follow a specific topic.

URL—(Universal Resource Locator) The Internet address of a web page.

Copyright Credits

Web sites used in this book have been used with permission of the creators and/or webmasters. Thanks go to these sites for providing educators with resources for use in their classrooms. Specific credits go to these sites:

Excite Search Web site: Excite, Excite Search and the Excite Logo are trademarks of Excite, Inc. and may be registered in various jurisdictions. Excite screen display copyright 1995—1999 Excite, Inc.

Special thanks to the contributors to *MidLink Magazine*. Schools and students from around the world provide all of these projects and activities.

The Virtual Polyhedra Web site is the property of George Hart, http://www.li.net/~george.

The Ask Jeeves for Kids! Web site is used by permission of Ask Jeeves, Inc., Berkeley, CA, USA, copyright Ask Jeeves, Inc. 1997-1998, all rights reserved. "Ask Jeeves" and "Ask Jeeves for Kids!" are trademarks of Ask Jeeves, Inc.

Neuroscience for Kids Web site was used with permission of Dr. Eric H. Chudler, Neuroscience for Kids, http://weber.u.washington.edu/~chudler/neurok.html.

Jan Brett Web site and all artwork are copyright Jan Brett.

Yahoo! Inc., 3420 Central Expressway, 2nd Floor, Santa Clara, CA 95051.

Index

Index *(cont.)*